FUNDAMENTAL DOCTRINES

UNDERSTANDING THE ELEMENTARY PRINCIPLES OF CHRIST

MICHAEL BOLDEA, JR.

BOLDMAN PUBLISHING
WATERTOWN, WISCONSIN

Published by:

Boldman Publishing
Watertown, Wisconsin
http://www.handofhelp.com

ISBN: 9780615680477

For all who hunger after truth.

~MB

ISAIAH 28:9-10, "WHOM WILL HE TEACH KNOWLEDGE? AND WHOM WILL HE MAKE TO UNDERSTAND THE MESSAGE? THOSE JUST WEANED FROM MILK? THOSE JUST DRAWN FROM THE BREASTS? FOR PRECEPT MUST BE UPON PRECEPT UPON PRECEPT, LINE UPON LINE UPON LINE, HERE A LITTLE, THERE A LITTLE."

CHAPTER ONE
INTRODUCTION

It has been said that a house is only as solid as the foundation upon which it stands. One can build a magnificent home and use the best materials, but if the foundation is not stable and firm, and not as the architect designed it to be, no matter how grandiose the edifice, it will soon come crumbling to the ground. Foundations are important. This is why one begins by laying the foundation of any new building, and then proceeds to build the walls upon the foundation.

Just as any home requires a stable foundation, our life of faith and our doctrinal beliefs require a stable foundation. So many today find themselves in the position of building their spiritual home without ever having built a firm foundation, and whether it's in six months or six years into the future, serious problems begin to arise that endanger the entire construct of their faith.

Throughout my years of ministry, and they are not few, I have seen the faith of many souls shipwrecked due to the lack of a spiritual foundation. I must forewarn you this will be a Biblically centered rather than a denominationally centered book, one I believe is necessary and vital, especially given the times of confusion and spiritual ignorance in which we are living.

One cannot have a good end if they do not have a good beginning. One cannot finish the race faithfully, if one began the race on the wrong footing, and is headed in the wrong direction. Yes, the foundational teachings, and the fundamental doctrines of our Christian faith, are as necessary today as they ever were, and every generation has the duty and responsibility to make certain that the foundation is sound, well-grounded in the Word, stable, and secure in Christ.

As a backdrop to this entire volume, we will be using a Scripture passage out of the epistle to the Hebrews that consists of no more than three verses.

Hebrews 6:1-3, "Therefore, leaving the discussion of the elementary principles of Christ, let us go on to perfection, not laying again the foundation of repentance from dead works and of faith toward God, of the doctrine of baptisms, of laying on of hands, of resurrection of the dead, and of eternal judgment. And this we will do if God permits."

What the writer of Hebrews is attempting to convey through these three verses is that these elementary principles of Christ he is referring to, and goes on to enumerate, must constitute the foundation of our faith, and our spiritual lives. His message to the Hebrews, as well as to us all was as simple as it was concise. You cannot grow in your faith, you cannot make progress, and you cannot build your spiritual house, until you have first laid this foundation. Only after these things have been established in your heart, and only after this foundation has settled in your spirit can you go on to perfection. These fundamental truths, these elementary principles of Christ cannot be bypassed, they cannot be ignored, nor can they be dismissed, because they are the foundation of our faith upon which we build the entire construct of our spiritual lives.

Paul is saying to the Hebrews that they had already laid this foundation. They had already learned the elementary principles of Christ, and now that these things had been established in them it was time for them to go on to perfection. And this, Paul said, they would do if God permitted.

God's desire is that the foundation be established in the hearts of believers, so they might then go on to perfection. One cannot go on to perfection however, unless the foundation is first and foremost firmly established. I realize full well that by now some of you are thinking to yourselves, that you are far too mature in your faith to sit there and read a book about the elementary principles of Christ, but no matter how mature we are in our faith it is always good to reacquaint ourselves with these things, to inspect our foundation, see that it is still as stable as ever, and built upon the rock which is Christ Jesus.

In doing the research for this book, and reacquainting myself with these elementary principles of Christ, I too discovered some fresh insight, some nuggets of truth, and some new wisdom that had been dulled by the passage of time from when I first laid my foundation of faith.

So what are these fundamental teachings that we will be discussing throughout this book? We will be discussing those things which Paul listed as being the elementary principles of Christ, and we will do so in the order he listed them beginning with repentance from dead works, continuing on to faith toward God, the doctrine of baptisms, (such as the baptism of John, the baptism unto repentance, the baptism of Christ, the baptism with the Holy Spirit,) continuing further still with the laying on of hands, the resurrection of the dead, and concluding with eternal judgment.

What I find amazing is that Paul lists these doctrines and then proceeds to define them as elementary principles of Christ. Now we all know that the word elementary is defined as basic, essential or fundamental. The term elementary constitutes the simplest aspects of a subject in fact. So these things that Paul lists as the elementary principles of Christ are the basic, essential, and fundamental doctrines that every believer should have squared away, and established in his heart as a foundation for the spiritual life of holiness and righteousness unto God they ought to live. In other words, these principles of Christ, elementary as they might be, are a necessary foundation for every believer. One cannot build a spiritual house, if this foundation is not firmly established.

I needed to get that point across because, for some unexplained reason, doctrines such as repentance, faith toward God, eternal judgment and baptisms are rarely discussed in the church as though they were unnecessary or a hindrance in the way of the vastly more relevant topics of positive thinking, dynamic self-esteem, or balancing your checkbook in four easy steps.

There are numerous passages in Scripture wherein the Christian walk and a life in Christ are readily compared with building a house, and no other Biblical author does it more frequently than the apostle Paul. Perhaps it is due to the fact that he himself was a tentmaker that Paul makes so many references to a spiritual life being comparable to a house, but whatever the reason, the comparisons he draws are truly remarkable and awe inspiring.

1 Corinthians 3:9-11, "For we are God's fellow workers; you are God's field, you are God's building. According to the grace of God which was given to me, as a wise master builder I have laid the foundation, and another builds on it. But let each one take heed how he builds on it. For no other foundation can anyone lay than that which is laid, which is Jesus Christ."

Ephesians 2:19-22, "Now, therefore, you are no longer strangers and foreigners, but fellow citizens with the saints and members of the household of God, having been built on the foundation of the apostles and prophets, Jesus Christ Himself being the chief cornerstone, in whom the whole building, being joined together, grows into a holy temple in the Lord, in whom you also are being built together for a habitation of God in the Spirit."

There are some powerful truths that we must highlight in what Paul the Apostle wrote both to the Corinthians as well as the Ephesians. First, to the Corinthians he declares that there is only one foundation. No matter what the house will look like once it is done, the foundation must always be the same when it comes to our spiritual homes, and that foundation must always, and without exception be Christ Jesus. Paul even goes so far as to assert that no other foundation can anyone else lay than that which is laid, which is Jesus Christ.

If our spiritual journey does not begin with Christ and in Christ, then we've started off on the wrong path. If our foundation is not Christ, if it is not rooted in the truth of God's Word, if the cornerstone of our temple is not Jesus, then we are tilting at windmills, and are among all men most pitiable.

It is this foundation of Christ Jesus that makes us fellow citizens with the saints, members of the household of God, and no longer strangers and foreigners. It is only in Christ that we are deemed able to be built together for a habitation of God in the Spirit.

It is only in Christ that we can have the life of God flowing through us, and in us.

Lest we believe it was only Paul that used the metaphor of a house or that of building a house when referring to our spiritual growth, maturity, and foundation, the Apostle Peter also spent some time on this topic both making references to the individual being as a living stone, as well as quoting a passage from the book of Isaiah, in reference to Jesus the chief cornerstone.

1 Peter 2:4-6, "Coming to Him as to a living stone, rejected indeed by men, but chosen by God and precious, you also, as living stones are being built up a spiritual house, a holy priesthood, to offer up spiritual sacrifices acceptable to God through Jesus Christ."

Throughout the Word of God and especially in the New Testament, we see the importance placed on the foundation of a thing, be it the foundational principles of God, or the elementary principles of Christ. Every author of Scripture stresses the importance of knowing these things, of being able not only to understand them, but also to explain them further. Some of the topics that Paul defines as elementary principles are not so elementary for many in our modern age, tragically even for those calling themselves preachers and teachers of God's Holy Word. It always astounds me that men we judge somehow inferior in intelligence when compared to those of our modern age, had a firmer grasp on the important and relevant matters of a true spiritual life – understanding what were to them the elementary principles of Christ – while we, in our modern enlightened age, struggle with such doctrines as the resurrection of the dead, or eternal judgment.

I have more than one hypothesis as to why men we might consider ignorant by today's standards were, in fact, far wiser when it came to spiritual things than our present generation. At the top of the list is nothing more than modern idolatry. We've become so caught up in this present life, so focused on the material things of this world, we've allowed, without much inner struggle, God to be set aside and thus we've lost sight of what truly matters... that there is a hereafter, and there is an eternity beckoning to us all with every breath we take.

Let's be honest. There are countless souls today paying God lip service. There are thousands upon thousands of men and women raising a limp hand in the air at a crusade just for fire insurance. All the while these selfsame individuals are thinking that if there is a hell, and if there is a heaven, well, it won't hurt to just raise their hand and walk up the aisle.

Our indifference toward the things of God, as a generation, betrays our true heart. It betrays the fact that we take a sovereign, omnipotent God all too lightly, and that we would prefer it if God would just sit in a corner somewhere and wait on us to call on Him when we need His help. Other than that, we would surely appreciate it if He wouldn't interfere or otherwise intrude on our lives, and/or take our advice about how things ought to be handled.

The elementary principles of Christ, elementary, basic things that every believer ought to know, include such doctrines as the doctrine of repentance, the doctrine of the resurrection of the dead, the doctrine of eternal judgments, baptisms, and faith unto God. Elementary! I cannot stress this word enough. These are elementary principles; foundational principles every believer ought to be familiar with, and know, and live. I fear we have oversimplified the Christian walk. I am not referring to salvation itself, but the intricacies of the Christian walk, as an ongoing transformation and molding of an individual. We are reticent in probing deeper when it comes to daily growth in God, that daily growth in wisdom, and in power, in knowledge and in understanding which comes only by way of a solid relationship and an intimacy with God. We have grown complacent. We have grown comfortable with not growing, with not maturing, and we are content to remain in a static state, not realizing that the longer we remain static the more lethargic we become, and the easier we will be to overtake.

We tend to forget that we have an enemy, and this enemy will go to any length just so he could devour us, cause us to stumble, and cause us to fall. The enemy we face is cunning, and he has been perfecting his craft over millennia. There is one other thing we must acknowledge concerning this enemy of ours, the fact that his time is short. He knows his time is short, and he knows that we know his time is short, and now is his final push, his last ditch effort to take as many captives as he can.

This is why our foundation is important, this is why we must know the elementary principles of Christ, because a sure foundation will ensure a sure footing, and a sure footing will ensure that we are established in Christ. The true Christian life begins only once we've encountered Christ personally, intimately, and directly. Once we've encountered Him it is impossible to remain the same and unchanged.

Paul was writing to the Hebrews and was in essence saying to them: *'look, we've gone over this, we've already established the elementary principles of Christ, we've already laid the doctrinal foundation of what you ought to believe, and rather than continue building from there, rather than go on to perfection, I am forced to reacquaint you with things such as the doctrine of baptisms, the doctrine of repentance, the doctrine of laying on of hands, because you did not grow, you did not go beyond the foundation, but rather you allowed the foundation to come to ruination in that you did not persist and persevere in the Word and the doctrines that were established in your midst.'*

My hope and my prayer is that this book will help you grow in Christ. That's it! I have no grandiose hopes for this volume of teachings, other than to establish you in the truth of God's Word, and to help you grow in Jesus. If I achieve this goal, if I achieve this objective, then I will have considered all my efforts, all the time away from my family, and all the hours it took to put this book together, worthwhile. There is a verse in Hosea that has always troubled me on a very basic level.

It is Hosea 4:6, and the verse begins with a declaration made by none other than God, which states: *"My people are destroyed for lack of knowledge."*

But how could we be lacking in knowledge? We have access to countless sources of information at our fingertips, the world is more plugged in and more aware than ever before, there is a larger cross section of the population that is able to access unimaginable quantities of books and teaching materials, how could we be lacking in knowledge?

The knowledge that God speaks of is knowledge of His Word, His will, His nature, and His presence in our lives. It is not necessarily book knowledge, but rather knowledge of Him, and yes,

I can attest to the fact that countless souls are destroyed for lack of knowledge of God. The knowledge God speaks of in Hosea includes the elementary principles of Christ that Paul speaks of in Hebrews. It is a necessary knowledge, a knowledge that keeps us and protects us, growing us from strength to strength and from grace to grace.

So how important is this knowledge of Christ? How important is this knowledge of the elementary principles of Christ? How important is this knowledge of the will of God? The answer in a word: paramount. Eternity itself hinges on the knowledge we possess. For some, whom God defines as His people, are destroyed for lack of knowledge. These, dear friends, were not infidels that were being destroyed for lack of knowledge, they were not of the tribes of the gentiles, these were people whom God called His people, yet they too were destroyed for lack of knowledge. Knowledge of the will of God, knowledge of the elementary principles of Christ, these things are paramount in the life of the believer, far more important and necessary than learning how to turn your frown upside down, or putting on a happy face even when you're crying on the inside. Too much focus is being placed on the physical, on the now, on the temporal, on this passing, fleeting thing we call life on planet earth, and all too readily the eternal and lasting things of God are summarily ignored or dismissed.

There are other Scriptures that reveal the truth of how important this knowledge is to us and for us. For the sake of brevity, I will only go through two of them, but I assure you there are many more within the Bible that make the undeniable correlation and connection between knowledge and eternity.

John 17:3, "And this is eternal life, that they may know You, the only true God, and Jesus Christ whom You have sent."

1 John 5:13, "These things I have written to you who believe in the name of the Son of God, that you may know that you have eternal life, and that you may continue to believe in the name of the Son of God."

Lord willing, throughout this journey we will amass knowledge. We will reacquaint ourselves with the foundation of our faith, and the elementary principles of Christ, so we might be complete Christians, in complete authority, able stand with boldness and courage undeterred by the slings and arrows of the enemy. The enemy loves ignorance and he revels in it, because an ignorant Christian does not know the measure of his strength or authority in Christ, and so succumbs to the onslaught of the enemy's tactics. We will amass not the knowledge of man which perishes or is rendered irrelevant, but the knowledge of God which is as lasting as God Himself, thereby becoming aware of that which we have access to in Jesus.

REPENTANCE IS TURNING AWAY
FROM A PREVIOUS PRACTICE,
NEVER AGAIN TO RETURN TO IT.
REPENTANCE IS NOT A FEELING
OF REMORSE OR REGRET FOR THE
SINS YOU HAVE COMMITTED, BUT
AN ACTUAL TURNING AWAY FROM
SAID SIN, AND NEVER REVISITING
IT AGAIN.

CHAPTER TWO
REPENTANCE

The idea for this book emerged one day while I was reading the sixth chapter of the epistle to the Hebrews. As I read what the author described as the elementary principles of Christ, I realize that these elementary principles – these basic doctrines, these teachings, which ought to be the foundation of our faith – are only rarely, if ever taught in today's modern churches. I felt in my heart that there was a need to reacquaint ourselves with the elementary principles of Christ, once more, and went to work putting this book together.

What I found intriguing is that Paul begins with repentance, or repentance from dead works, as the first of the elementary principles of Christ, and ends with eternal judgment. So within the span of three verses Paul lays out the entirety of the Christian experience, from the first step, that of repentance, to the last, that of eternal judgment for the disobedient, rebellious and unregenerate.

So what is repentance? In its most basic definition, repentance is turning away from a previous practice, never again to return to it. Repentance is not a feeling of remorse or regret for the sins you have committed but an actual turning away from said sin, and never revisiting it again. I meet many people who tell me that they've repented of a sin only to fall back into that selfsame sin again. Then, my friend, it wasn't true repentance. It was perhaps a feeling of shame, of regret, of remorse, but if it had been true repentance you would have never gone back to that sin or practice again.

Why should we preach and teach repentance? The simple answer is because Jesus taught and preached repentance, as did John the Baptist, as did Paul and every disciple of Christ that is included in the Bible. Even before the advent of Christ, the heart of God was for His people to repent, and turn back to Him that He might bless them rather than judge them, that He might comfort them rather than punish them.

Repentance is the first step in our spiritual journey; a journey that lasts our entire lives here on earth. Throughout this journey we are taken from grace to grace, and from strength to strength. It is a process. One cannot achieve maturity in Christ, possess spiritual gifts, or know the fullness of the joy and peace God brings, unless they have first and foremost gone through the process of repentance.

Repentance is interwoven and is, in fact, a prerequisite of God throughout Scriptures. There is a verse that I hear quoted very often in many churches, but it also seems to be one of the most misunderstood verses in the church as well. In fact this one verse lays out what repentance truly is, and the steps one must follow in order to achieve it.

2 Chronicles, 7:14, "If My people who are called by My name will humble themselves and pray, and seek My face, and turn from their wicked ways, then I will hear from heaven, and will forgive their sin and heal their land."

The shorthand version of this verse could readily be, 'if My people, who are called by My name repent, then I will hear from heaven and will forgive their sin and heal their land.' Within this one word repentance, we see a handful of actions that must take place. First, in order to experience true repentance one must humble one's self. Second, one must pray and seek God's face, and third, turn from one's wicked ways. Saying sorry is not enough, and no, saying sorry isn't the hardest thing on the list. Remorse is easy when we see our entire life come crumbling to the ground around us. When the consequences of our sins have caught up to us, and what once seemed sweet to the taste is now bitter, what once seemed pleasing to the eye, is now grotesque and off putting, remorse comes naturally.

There are two things on this list that people seem to have trouble doing, the first is truly humbling themselves, and the second is turning from their wicked ways. We live in a day and age wherein humility and humbling oneself are viewed as a weakness rather than strength. We are taught, even within our churches to be self-assured and self-empowered, to view ourselves in a positive light, to see ourselves not as we truly are, but as something bigger, better, and stronger.

Humility, in its purest definition, is to abase the pride and arrogance of self, and make oneself meek and submissive. Humility is acknowledging our shortcomings and failures as well as acknowledging our need for a Savior. We like to think we are strong; we like to think we can do it on our own, but it is this mindset that keeps many slaves to sin and vice, because they never cry out, they never humble themselves seeking the face of God, asking for His help and guidance.

Repentance also requires a turning from our wicked ways. The fact that we visit our sin less frequently than before is not good enough, neither is the fact that we might not find as much pleasure in sin as we once did. Repentance is a turning away, a separation from, and a renunciation of our wicked ways. Repentance is to stop in your tracks, make a hundred and eighty degree turn, and head in the opposite direction.

In order to understand why such drastic measures are necessary when it comes to sin, we must first understand the destructive power of sin. Sin separates man from God. It separates man from the grace of God, it separates man from the peace of God, and it separates man from the will of God. One cannot have sin of which they have not repented in their heart, and yet presume to walk in the will of God. It is an impossibility for one to be in God's will, without first having humbled one's self, sought His face, prayed, and turned from one's wicked way.

When this occurs in the life of an individual, when true repentance takes hold, their life is utterly transformed. Repentance is the genesis of a new life in God. We are given a new heart, a new mind, new desires, and a new focus. We are no longer what we once were, we no longer desire what we once desired, but are made new creatures in Him.

In the twelfth chapter of Hebrews, beginning with the sixteenth verse, Paul the Apostle highlights the danger of not turning from our wicked ways, but continuing in our sin absent of repentance. He speaks of Esau, the brother of Jacob, who sold his birthright for a morsel of food, then pens something truly remarkable.

Hebrews 12:17, "For you know that afterward, when he wanted to inherit the blessing, he was rejected, for he found no place for repentance, though he sought it diligently with tears."

When taking into account that Esau forfeited his entire future, and all that the inheritance of the blessing would have meant for him for a bowl of lentil stew, it is no wonder that he sought repentance both diligently, and with tears, but repentance could not be found. A missed opportunity, a lost opportunity, is lost forever. One never relives the exact same moment in their existence, and one cannot go back and remedy the wrong and foolish choices that they made. A man can paint a picture of a million blades of grass, but he cannot make one of those blades of grass real. What does this have to do with repentance?

Well, a man can let many opportunities for repentance pass him by, a man can ignore many opportunities to repent, but he can never create an opportunity for repentance on his own. It is God, working through the Holy Spirit that creates the opportunity and environment for our moment of repentance, our moment of being transformed, and it is at that moment that we must humble ourselves and receive the gift of grace from the hand of God. We do not repent when we think it an opportune moment, or when we consider that it is a good season in our lives, but when God calls us to repentance... when the opportunity is presented to us. Repentance in the heart of man is the work of God. Of this there can be no doubt. There is one thing that God requires of man, one thing that man must do, and that is to submit and surrender to the truth. When we persist in our disobedience, when we dismiss opportunity after opportunity to repent and turn to God, there may come that frightful day when we, as Esau, will seek to find repentance with diligence and tears but for us it will be too late.

One of the enemy's greatest ploys is to convince men to forfeit their future for a moment in the present. It is exactly what happened to Esau. Herein lays the beauty of faith, for faith is the mystery that plucks you from the arms of the present, a present wrought with sin and despair, and translates you into the future that as yet you cannot see.

No one is exempt from the requirement of repentance! I cannot put it any plainer than that. No one can bypass repentance and still claim to have a relationship with Christ!

Repentance is such an important element in our spiritual growth, that Christ, John the Baptist, Peter, and Paul called men to repentance first and foremost.

In the gospel according to Matthew, we see John the Baptist preaching in the wilderness of Judea saying, 'repent, for the kingdom of heaven is at hand!'

As many of the Pharisees and Sadducees came to his baptism, John the Baptist addressed them, not in a soothing loving fashion, not with a church organ playing 'just as I am' in the background, but rather with a harsh rebuke.

Matthew 3:7-8, "But when he saw many of the Pharisees and Sadducees coming to his baptism he said to them, 'Brood of vipers! Who has warned you to flee from the wrath to come? Therefore bear fruits worthy of repentance."

The Pharisees and Sadducees wanted the baptism of John, absent of the requisite repentance, and his question to them was 'who has warned you to flee from the wrath to come?' He then goes on to open their eyes to the reality that absent repentance, baptism is just dipping oneself in water fully clothed, and nothing more. He admonishes them to bear fruits worthy of repentance first, and then come for baptism.

In the next chapter of Matthew, Jesus begins His preaching ministry, by echoing the selfsame words that John the Baptist spoke in the previous chapter.

Matthew 4:17, "From that time Jesus began to preach and to say, 'repent, for the kingdom of heaven is at hand."

Why did all the pillars of the faith including Jesus Himself preach repentance? Why is repentance such an important aspect of our Christian walk, and why was it named among the elementary principles of Christ? There is no better answer to this question, than the one that Paul gives to the learned men and philosophers of Athens, as he delivers his sermon on Mar's Hill, confounding the wisest men of that time:

Acts 17:30-31, "Truly, these times of ignorance God overlooked, but now commands all men everywhere to repent, because He has appointed a day on which He will judge the world in righteousness by the Man whom He has ordained. He has given assurance of this to all by raising Him from the dead."

So why repent? Because God has appointed a day on which He will judge the world in righteousness, by the man whom He has ordained. This Man is none other than the Christ, and absent repentance, the righteousness of God will constrain Him to judge us together with the world. There is another aspect of this passage that is worth delving into, and that is the fact that God commands all men, everywhere to repent. Not just some men, not just men from a certain bloodline, nation or denomination, all men, everywhere. Young or old, rich or poor, wise man or fool, all men everywhere are commanded to repent. Whether we submit, humble ourselves, and obey God's command, is entirely on our shoulders.

The message has not changed over the centuries. The message has remained the same, and has withstood the test of time. Repent! Repent, for the kingdom of heaven is at hand. Men have attempted to sugar coat it, to make it more palatable, some have even attempted to remove it from among the elementary principles of Christ altogether, because it requires change on our part, and that isn't very popular nowadays.

Too many want to remain in their sin, tethered to their vices, and still enjoy all the benefits of son ship. Too many want to have one foot in the world and another in the church, not because they desire a true and lasting relationship with Christ, but to have something akin to preemptive fire insurance. Attending a church service, or becoming a member of a given denomination without true repentance, will do absolutely nothing to bring you into a right standing with God. I realize that self-deception is a powerful tool and many employ it liberally, but the truth is self-sustaining, and it will not conform itself to the times, or to men's whims.

Romans 12:2, "And do not be conformed to this world, but be transformed by the renewing of your mind, that you may prove what is that good and acceptable and perfect will of God."
This was Paul's admonition to the Romans, and it remains his admonition to us all. Just because a certain viewpoint is widely accepted by the world does not make it right or true. Like it or not, salvation begins with forgiveness, which comes only after repentance.

Nowadays, rather than preach repentance, (the selfsame repentance that was preached by Christ and echoed by all His apostles), we are told to believe only, and everything will be well and good. But it is repentance that produces in us a transformed mind, a transformed heart, a transformed will, and transformed desires. In essence when a soul repents, it turns away from sin and toward God. We cannot possess faith, nor can we have faith in Christ, if we have not firstly experienced true repentance.

As Paul was bidding farewell to the Ephesian elders in the book of Acts, in the twentieth chapter, he encourages his fellow brothers in Christ by telling them that he had kept nothing back from them that was helpful, but proclaimed repentance toward God and faith toward our Lord Jesus Christ to them. We repent away from sin, but toward God. As I heard it said once, true repentance is the unyielding desire not to break God's heart. It's not feeling remorse because you got caught doing something you were not supposed to, it is a turning away from sin, and from the world, that we would not break God's heart anymore. Yes, repentance is a turning, a transformation, a change that is vital, crucial, and necessary for everyone who desires to walk according to the will of God.

Everyone needs repentance. There are no exemptions, no special passes, and no exclusions. There is a pervasive mentality among some believers that says one need only repent if they were truly wicked before coming to Christ. As such, there are some who feel they have no need of repentance because they didn't steal, they didn't murder, and they didn't commit any 'really bad sins'. When Paul enumerates the elementary principles of Christ, he makes certain to underline the fact that he is not speaking only of repentance from sin, but also repentance from dead works. If the wellspring of our efforts, works, deeds and actions is not Christ Jesus, then even the most giving, charitable, and generous works we can perform are dead, and have no value in and of themselves. Works will not get us into heaven, only grace and Christ will. 'So are you saying we shouldn't be generous and benevolent? Are you saying we shouldn't give?' No, that is not what I am saying.

What I am saying is that we do not do works in order to be saved; we do works because we are saved. We do not do works in order to be saved, as though by our works we might obtain salvation, but rather because we are saved, we are compelled by the nature of Christ in us to works of righteousness. Being saved is having the heart of Christ, and having the heart of Christ compels us to reach out to the hurting, the hungry, the forsaken and the forgotten.

The program can be entertaining, the pastor can be eloquent, the sermon engaging and humorous, but if repentance is not the central theme, if remission of sins in His name is not preached, if Christ is not preeminent and glorified, then it was all wasted time. Yes, it might make the flesh feel a little better, especially if it's a message about being positive, or having good self-esteem, but in the end, when all is said and done, the hollowness remains, for the essence of the message was something other than Christ.

No doubt repentance will never be popular, it will never draw the big crowds, it will never be what the majority want to hear, but it is what they need to hear. Absent of falling on our face at the foot of the cross, absent of true repentance – the repentance that transforms a man from the inside out – we will never know the fullness of God, nor the fullness of His power.

When I first started out in ministry, I made a vow to God that I would preach the gospel of Christ in its entirety, and that I would focus on the essential doctrines that are largely being ignored in the contemporary church. I also vowed that I would not sugar coat harsh truths just to spare feelings.

So here is a harsh but a necessary truth: Religiosity will not save your soul. Great entertainment will not save your soul. Throwing a hand up in the air at a crusade but never really being transformed, never really experiencing repentance will not save your soul. Only humbling yourself, falling at the foot of the cross, and repenting, turning away from your old life, and turning toward God can save your soul. Unpopular stand? Unequivocally yes. Biblically sound? Unequivocally yes.

All I can do is share truth with you. Is this your opportunity to receive it? If you do not, will you be granted another time?

FAITH IS THE SPIRITUAL SUBSTANCE, THE SPIRITUAL CONDUIT BY WHICH WE CAN HAVE A CONNECTION WITH GOD AND HIS UNSEEN, UNFATHOMABLE KINGDOM.

CHAPTER THREE
FAITH

The second principle on Paul's list is an oft misunderstood, infrequently accessed, fundamentally necessary element of the Christian experience. Faith. No matter how beautiful a building, if the foundation is not built to specifications or if the foundation is weak, it is only a matter of time before it all comes crumbling to the ground.

Although it might not seem like it at first glance, the doctrine of faith toward God is both deep and wide. It is by no means shallow, and there is much to discuss when it comes to the topic of faith. As an introduction to the doctrine of faith toward God, we will begin by addressing the nature of faith.

Although there is a plethora of ideas, doctrines, formulations and hypothesis concerning faith in the world, we will focus exclusively on what the Word of God has to say about it. Even those who do not know God, who have no relationship or fellowship with Him, use the term faith, but the faith they possess is not saving faith, for there is only one saving faith, and that is in Christ Jesus through what He did for us on the cross.

True faith has its origins, its roots, and its power in the Word of God. Thus the reason we must go to the Word in order to discover the nature of faith, and more importantly how to appropriate this faith in our daily lives that we might grow, mature, and become those faithful servants which God can use and work with and through.

There is no more succinct and in-depth definition of faith in the entire Bible than the one we find in the eleventh chapter of the epistle to the Hebrews. In fact, it is the only passage in Scripture that outright defines faith.

Hebrews 11:1, *"Now faith is the substance of things hoped for, the evidence of things not seen."*

The operative words in this powerful Scripture are substance and evidence.

So what is substance?

In its simplest definition, substance is defined as the invariable matter of which a person or a thing exists. Substance is matter...it is essence. In other words, faith is a sure and quantifiable work of the grace of God that is both felt and seen. Faith is a spiritual reality by which we can enter in to other spiritual realities. Faith is the doorway into the gifts and promises of God. It is the foundation, the substance, placed in us by God that we might attain those things that are out of reach for the human mind. Faith is the faculty, or the gift that perceives the unseen things that cover the entire spectrum of spiritual reality. It is by no means an intellectual or human faculty. Faith is the spiritual substance, the spiritual conduit by which we can have a connection with God and His unseen, unfathomable kingdom.

Spiritual substance exists, and it is as real as the material substance that surrounds us.

Just as our senses put us in touch with the physical world, faith puts us in touch with the spiritual. There is another nugget of truth that is worth mentioning, and that is just as our sense of sight is employed when there is light, and our sense of hearing when there is sound, faith is employed in perceiving the unseen and eternal.

By its very definition faith is very different from hope. There are some who would readily interchange faith and hope, but true faith goes far beyond what hope can carry us. Faith is certainty, and this certainty gives us the boldness to press on. Another glaring difference between faith and hope is that while hope is anchored in future things, faith is steadfastly anchored in the present. When one hopes, they merely desire that some thing, or some wish, will be fulfilled at a future date. When we have faith however, we walk in certitude, for faith is the evidence of things not seen.

Hope is an attitude of expectation, while faith is something real that has been placed in us for the present, for this time, and not some future time.

It is also important to note that the significant difference between hope and faith is that faith resides in the heart of man. Faith is an issue of the heart, while hope resides in the mind of a man, and is an issue of human reasoning.

The apostle Paul himself asserts this truth, and poetically so when encouraging the church of Thessalonica.

1 Thessalonians 5:8, "But let us who are of the day be sober, putting on the breastplate of faith and love, and as a helmet the hope of salvation."

It is common knowledge that while a breastplate covers the chest, and the heart, a helmet covers the head. This is not to imply that hope is wrong. Hope is a glorious virtue, but we cannot confuse it or interchange it with faith. Hope comes from the mind of man, but faith springs up from the heart of man. Both have distinct and purposeful origins.

When faith is present in the heart of an individual, this faith toward God produces change. A faith that does not produce change, is no faith at all, and is merely hope that has been misinterpreted as faith. Faith produces transformation, it produces change, and we cannot possess true faith without being thoroughly transformed in our hearts.

Another way of looking at it is that faith produces fruit. One can claim to have faith, but if they have no fruit, then it is merely a claim. The Apostle James even goes so far as to say that faith by itself, if it does not have works, is dead. Faith is action, and absent of action, we either have a hope that is made up to look like faith, or a dead faith that does nothing to transform.

James 2:8, "But someone will say, 'You have faith, and I have works.' Show me your faith without your works, and I will show you my faith by my works."

Faith is not the logical acceptance of a thing. Faith is not mental agreement. Faith is transformative, and it begins in the hearts of man. Faith leads us to faith, and is received by faith.

Once again, we defer to the Apostle Paul who this time is writing to the Romans, and in the context of talking about the gospel of Christ, and the fact that it is the power of God to salvation for everyone who believes, also says something truly profound about faith.

Romans 1:16-17, "For I am not ashamed of the gospel of Christ for it is the power of God to salvation for everyone who believes, for the Jew first and also for the Greek. For in it the righteousness of God is revealed from faith to faith; as it is written, 'The just shall live by faith."

In other words, once the righteousness of God is revealed to us through the Scriptures, it leads us to faith, but not only that, the faith to which the Scripture leads us will invariably lead us to greater faith still. We grow from faith to faith in Christ, having the gospel of Christ, which is the power of God to salvation for those who believe, as the spark that begins our transformation.

Once we receive the righteousness of God by faith, it propels us to greater faith, until we come to that point wherein we echo Habakkuk just as Paul did, and say 'the just shall live by faith'.

Faith so changes your life, your emotions, your thoughts and your desires, that you come to the point of living by faith. Faith is not something we practice on the weekends, nor is faith something we employ only when we are among the brethren. Faith is not something we plug into only when we're in trouble. Faith is a way of life. That is true and saving faith.

I realize that in our modern culture, with all its trappings and distractions it might seem odd, even strange, to speak about or encourage living by faith. It is not I who is encouraging this however, but rather the Word of God is encouraging it. Yes, the just shall live by faith. What a marvelous thing.

For some even the thought of living by faith is anathema, and taboo, because they are still tethered to this world, and their hearts and minds are firmly anchored in this present age. They do not understand that to live by faith is not a negative, but rather the greatest of positives. It is a glorious thing when one has grown from faith to faith, and has come to that place in their relationship and intimacy with God that they can live by faith, having full assurance that the Father, who sees all, will make a way in all things.

Faith toward God also operates in the present. We do not have faith that one day we will have salvation, but we have faith that we are presently saved. We do not have faith that one day we will have eternal life, but we have faith that we presently have eternal life.

As Jesus was speaking to a crowd that had gathered in the sixth chapter of the gospel according to John, He said something truly profound that sheds a greater light on what I am trying to convey.

John 6:47, "Most assuredly, I say to you, he who believes in Me has everlasting life."

Here we notice that Jesus did not use future tense, He did not say, 'most assuredly, I say to you, he who believes in Me will have everlasting life', but rather, 'he who believes in Me has everlasting life'. Faith is a present action, and it translates us into the kingdom and the promises of God. Eternal life works in us, here and now, and the power of eternal life is already operating in us. This is the beauty of faith...it works in the present.

Another characteristic of the nature of faith all believers should be aware of and acquainted with is that faith places its trust, and has as its foundation in the Word of God. The will of God, the mind of God, the plan of God for mankind, all are found within the Bible, His holy Word.

We were given faith that we might understand the kingdom of God, and see those things which are unseen by eyes of flesh. This faith, faith toward God, gives us access to this spiritual world, which, I would dare say, is more real than this present world. Why would I make such an assertion? Quite simply I can claim this because while the spiritual world is eternal, this world of ours, and everything in it, is passing away. Faith gives us spiritual eyes, and with eyes of faith we see the spiritual realm and the spiritual world that surrounds us.

Now when I say that a spiritual world surrounds us, it is by no means hyperbole or exaggeration. There is a real and present spiritual realm that surrounds us even now, and I can prove it Biblically.

In the book of second kings, there is an incident wherein the king of Syria sent horses, chariots, and a great army to surround the city that Elisha the prophet found himself in. At the time, Elisha had a servant with him, and this servant arose early and went out only to see this mass of humanity with chariots and horses surrounding them on all sides. Panicked, he returns to Elisha and says to him, "Alas my master! What shall we do?"

Elisha's answer was short, yet powerful in its implications. *"Do not fear, for those who are with us are more than those who are with them."* This was Elisha's answer even though the young man only saw the Syrian army that surrounded them, and nothing more.

I am certain the servant gave Elisha a disbelieving look, perhaps thinking to himself that the man was delusional. There was no one else there. What was he talking about? Where was this army that was on their side? The young servant only saw the Syrians.

Then something wondrous happened. Elisha prayed that his servant's eyes be opened, that he might see.

2 Kings 6:17, "And Elisha prayed, and said, 'Lord I pray, open his eyes that he may see.' Then the Lord opened the eyes of the young man, and he saw. And behold, the mountain was full of horses and chariots of fire all around Elisha."

The horses and chariots of fire were already there. The young man just didn't have the eyes to see them. The spiritual realm is all around us, but many – yes, even many who call themselves believers – don't have the spiritual eyes to see it. When I first received this revelation in my spirit it astounded me. The horses and chariots of fire were there already, it was the young man who could not peer into this reality. Elisha didn't pray *'Lord send some angels, Lord send some chariots of fire'*; he simply prayed that the eyes of his servant be open to the horses and chariots of fire that were already there.

This is what faith does. It opens our eyes to the spiritual realm, and the spiritual world that surrounds us that we might say as did Elisha, 'those who are with us are more than those who are with them'.

When we walk by faith and not by sight, we see beyond this present material world. There are so many instances in our lives when, if we were to walk by sight alone we would grow despondent and discouraged. Absent of faith we would look at our present circumstances we would look at our present trials, and be readily overcome by them. Faith however, allows us to see beyond what the eyes of flesh can see, and this gives us the assurance that if we run the race faithfully, if we remain steadfast and strong in our convictions, a crown of victory will be laid upon our heads.

Another wondrous beauty of faith toward God is that it can be ignited by just a single word. As Christ's disciples sat in a boat, tossed by the waves, in the middle of the sea, in the fourth watch of the night, they saw Jesus walking toward them. Some said it was a ghost and cried out in fear, but Jesus immediately calmed their spirits by encouraging them to be of good cheer, and informing them that it was He, and that they should not be afraid. Peter the Apostle of Christ was also among the disciples in the boat, and when he heard the voice of Christ he said, "Lord if it is You, command me to come to You on the water."

Then in Matthew fourteen, verse 29, Jesus simply says, 'Come' and Peter walked on the water to go to Jesus.

One word ignited Peter's faith; one word turned the laws of nature on their ear; one word nullified the law of gravitational attraction; Jesus only spoke one word to Peter, Jesus only said 'come' and Peter's faith was ignited. Once his faith was ignited, his faith took care of the rest.

For a while, Peter actually walked on water, but then he saw the wind and it was boisterous and so he became afraid. Peter took his eyes off Jesus, Peter allowed his fear to overwhelm his faith, and so he began to sink into the sea, and as he was sinking he cried out 'Lord save me!'

Matthew 14:31, "And immediately Jesus stretched out His hand and caught him, and said to him, 'O you of little faith, why did you doubt?"

Just consider that Christ's only rebuke was the lack of abundant faith in Peter's heart. Jesus didn't ask what made Peter think he could walk on water. He simply asked Peter why he doubted. 'O you of little faith, why did you doubt?'

The Word of God does not specify how many steps Peter took on the water, it doesn't specify how far he got from the boat, but at some point his faith wavered. At some point Peter saw himself standing upon the waves, he felt the wind upon his face, and his human mind began to reason that what he was doing was indeed impossible. *'Man can't walk on water'*, his mind screamed at him, and his faith was shut out.

If Jesus says 'come' do not let doubt steal away His promise toward you. If Jesus says 'come' even if it may seem impossible from a human perspective, even if all those around you would doubt the success of your endeavor, step out in faith, step upon the waves, and walk toward Him. Keep your eyes firmly planted upon Jesus, and let faith guide you toward His open arms.

So often we are afraid to step out in faith because, well, Peter began to sink didn't he? 'If Peter sank', we think to ourselves, 'we are sure to sink', all the while forgetting that Jesus was there. Even when Peter started to sink, Jesus stretched out his hand and caught him. Jesus will not let you sink! If your faith wavers, He will be there to stretch out His hand toward you, and catch you.

Before ending this chapter on faith, there is one more thing about the nature of faith toward God that I want to make crystal clear: Faith is not, and has nothing to do with positive thinking or positive affirmation. Nowhere in the Bible does it say that if you think positively, your faith will increase, or that if you affirm certain thing over and over again, that thing will be birthed into reality. Faith is a gift from God, and the Word of God activates it. We can pray for greater faith, we can ask God for greater faith, but we cannot manufacture greater faith.

Again, faith is a gift from God. When the gift of faith toward God is present in the heart, it exudes outwardly, and compels us to serve God, to worship God, to love God, and to obey God.

Although Paul might have seen faith as an elementary principle of Christ, it is this elementary principle, along with all the others we will be covering in this book, that we must reacquaint ourselves with as a people and as a generation, because we have strayed from the basic teachings and basic tenets of the faith, wandering in the wilderness, unaware of the fact that we are powerless and absent of direction, until it is too late.

While we are on the topic of faith, I would be remiss if I did not also address the relationship between faith and works. Yes, there is a relationship between faith and works, and it is a symbiotic one. As we make our way through the Word of God you will see the symmetry of these two ideas laid out in the Bible.

It is astounding to me that although Paul considered things such as repentance, faith toward God, and eternal judgment, just to name a few, elementary principles of Christ, an abundance of professing Christians today have not a clue as to these doctrines of the faith, or their importance and relevance in our daily lives.

There is always a danger when we substitute the necessary for the irrelevant, or as a popular cliché so aptly states, when we focus on the minor issues and dismiss the major ones. These elementary principles of Christ are the fundamentals of the faith. They are the bedrock, the foundation upon which our faith stands, and due to which is able to withstand the storms and trials of our spiritual walk. Ask any believer and they will tell you there are seasons of spiritual drought, spiritual hardships, and spiritual lack in this journey we call our walk of faith. Absent a sturdy foundation, absent a deeply rooted knowledge of the elementary principles of Christ, men's faith is inevitably shaken once a spiritual storm is unleashed.

Thus far we've established the definition of faith, and concluded that faith is the substance necessary for us as believers so we might see that which spiritual eyes only can see. Faith, in fact, is the evidence of things not seen and try as one might, no one can peer into that which is spiritual absent faith.

When all else is gone, when all else has abandoned us, faith keeps us and sustains us. Faith keeps us from desperation, faith keeps us from hopelessness, and faith gives us the assurance that as long as we remain in the will of God, He will be faithful in keeping us and protecting us.

When the Syrian army surrounded the city of Dothan, and Elisha's servant became fearful of them, Elisha did not pray for the Lord to send a bigger army, he did not pray to be supernaturally translated from the place he was in to another, he simply prayed that God open the eyes of his servant, so his servant might see what he already saw. The chariots of fire were already there, and the protectors of the righteous had already been dispatched. The only problem was the servant's perception. He had no eyes of faith, and only saw the Syrian army surrounding them. It was only when

Elisha prayed that God opened the servant's eyes, and he too saw what Elisha had been seeing all along.

Because he had eyes of faith, there was no doubt in Elisha. He knew that those who were with him far outnumbered the Syrian army. He knew that His protection was assured, and that God was on his side. Before his eyes were opened to the spiritual reality surrounding them, it was this selfsame servant who came to Elisha and said, 'Alas, my master! What shall we do?' having seen only the physical, having seen only the Syrian army and not the angelic hosts that had been dispatched to protect the man of God.

This is why faith is so important. It keeps us from being overwhelmed with fear and apprehension when we see the enemy's armies advancing against us. When the enemy advances and we possess faith, we see God's armies as well, with their chariots of fire all around us.

Faith is not hope; faith is assurance. When we say, 'I have faith that God will heal me', it is merely an expressed hope veiled as faith. When however we say 'I have faith that God has healed me', we are expressing a present assurance of an unseen event. This is the essence of faith; that we presently believe for that which we as yet do not see. We do not hope that Jesus will return; we are certain of it. Faith gives us the full assurance that one day we will see our beloved Savior in the clouds and in glory, returning for a spotless and undefiled bride.

There are many misconceptions within the church today in regards to the relationship between faith and works. What the Bible clearly describes as two symbiotic realities of the Christian walk, have become a point of contention among many a denomination, even though it ought not to be so.

The first and most important thing that we must understand about faith and works is that they are not mutually exclusive. Both faith and works work together toward a good end. They are symbiotic, and cannot be separated in the life of the believer, because once a believer has faith, his works will prove out his faith. Faith and works are like two sides of the same coin, both being part of the whole, both necessitating that they be visible in order for the whole to be complete.

I realize it is easier to say, 'I raised my hand in church once so I'm done, I'm good, I'm saved, redeemed, and on my way to heaven,' but when we begin to study and search out the Word of God and the hidden things of God, we realize that when we believe in Jesus, our lives must automatically change. We must, as a direct result of believing and receiving Jesus as Lord and Savior of our lives, be transformed into a new creature that goes about doing the things of the kingdom of God. If there is no fruit, no transformation, and no evidence that faith has indeed taken root in one's heart and as such compelled them to good works, then perhaps the individual merely had an experience, but was never really saved.

James 2:18-20, "But someone will say, 'You have faith, and I have works.' Show me your faith without your works, and I will show you my faith by my works. You believe that there is one God. You do well. Even the demons believe-and tremble. But do you want to know, O foolish man that faith without works is dead?"

Am I saying we are saved by works, or if having performed enough works can we be saved through them?

No. Works cannot save you, nor can works grant you entrance into the kingdom of God. Only faith can accomplish this. However, what I am saying is that faith proves itself by works. This is the selfsame thing that James said in his epistle.

I'm going to backtrack a little, and show you in the Word why I do not believe that man can be saved by works. I realize someone may be reading these words being under the misconception that if they simply do enough of something, they bypass faith in Jesus. 'I'm a good person, so I don't have to have that abiding faith in Jesus. I volunteer at a pet shelter, and give canned goods to the soup kitchen, so I don't have to believe in the birth, death, burial, and resurrection of Christ Jesus the Son of God. My simply being good, and doing good works, will earn me the right to enter the hallowed halls of heaven.'

This is the lie with which many attempt to soothe their burdened conscience, and though it might work for a season they soon discover it was, in fact, a lie.

Ephesians 2:4-9, "But God, who is rich in mercy, because of His great love with which He loved us, even when we were dead in trespasses, made us alive together with Christ, (by grace you have been saved), and raised us up together and made us sit together in the heavenly places in Christ Jesus, that in the ages to come He might show the exceeding riches of His grace in His kindness toward us in Christ Jesus. For by grace you have been saved through faith, and that not of yourselves; it is the gift of God, not of works, lest anyone should boast."

So did the Bible just contradict itself? We clearly have one passage that says that faith without works is dead, and another which says that we are saved through faith, and not of ourselves, and not of works lest anyone should boast.

No, the Bible did not contradict itself. We are saved through grace, by faith, yet faith proves itself by works.

Faith must be seen, it must be evident, the fruit of it must be visible to the naked eye, and God increases our faith that we might show it through the works that spring forth from our faith. God sees your works as the fruit of your faith, and men see your faith by your works.

As God considers nothing we do as good works lest it come from faith and through faith, men do not see my faith as a living, viable, and visible thing unless it is accompanied by works.

As James so adequately explains the works that spring forth from our faith, he poses a question to which we must give an answer as individuals.

James 2:15-16, "If a brother or a sister is naked and destitute of daily food, and one of you says to them, 'depart in peace, be warmed and filled', but you do not give them the things which are needed for the body, what does it profit?"

The answer is very clear. It profits nothing for us to tell someone who is hungry go and be filled, or someone who is naked go and be warmed, when our duty as children of God, as the heart, the hands and the feet of Christ is to go beyond words and help those who are in need, who are hurting, and who are suffering.

There is an imperious sense of self-righteousness I have often witnessed in some believers who insist works are unnecessary in the lives of Christians. Such individuals do not realize that every hungry person they meet, every needy person they encounter is an opportunity to show the love, the grace, and the mercy of Christ, and not merely talk about it.

There is something truly profound in what James says, when he says, 'I will show you my faith by my works.' This is the role of works in the lives of believers. By our works we show our faith.

I have often been asked why as a ministry we still focus so much on benevolence, on orphans and widows, on helping the poor and feeding the hungry.

'You yourself said you were called to preach the gospel, to encourage people to repentance, why all the other things?'

We do these things – feed the hungry, help the needy, care for the orphan, and clothe the naked – because by our works we show our faith. Rather than build my own kingdom, rather than amass for myself, my faith compels me to give as much as I can to those in need, to be the hands of Christ in a world that is growing increasingly indifferent, and to be the heart of Christ in a world that is growing increasingly heartless.

We do works not in order to be saved, but rather, we do works because we are saved. The new nature, the new mind, and the new heart, demand that we be the embodiment of Christ on this earth. We are His ambassadors, His representatives, and as such we must possess His heart.

There is a caveat to all this, something we need to discuss and flesh out, and that is, even though faith and works are symbiotic and they work together for a common good, faith is preeminent to works.

James 2:21-22, "Was not Abraham our father justified by works when he offered Isaac his son on the altar? Do you see that faith was working together with his works and by works faith was made perfect?"

I included both verses because I wanted you to understand the context, but what I want to focus on is the second part of this Scripture reading, wherein Jude points out that 'faith was working together with Abraham's works'. It is his faith that fueled his works, and not his works that fueled his faith. Yes, his faith was made perfect by works, but his works were not the instigator of his faith. Abraham had faith long before he was called to bring Isaac to mount Moriah, and because of his faith he followed through with action and did as God instructed. A faith that is not active, a faith that is not working, a faith that is not evident, is a dead faith. Faith is made perfect by works, when our works are fueled by our faith.

Between the writings of Paul and the writings of James we see the inward state of the regenerate man, the inward state of a man who has been reconciled unto God and sanctified through faith in Christ. We also see the outward state of a man who has been saved and redeemed. While Paul deals primarily with the inward part, the unseen things of man's nature, James deals with the outwardly manifestation of our inward faith, that which men must readily see in us if we are truly of Christ.

Paul details and outlines man in relation to God, digging deep into the spiritual implications of salvation by faith. James details and outlines man's relation to his contemporaries and fellow man. What we must understand is that we need both in order to be complete believers, ready for every good work. The inward condition has no worth without the outwardly manifestation thereof, just as the outwardly manifestation has no worth without the inward condition thereof. At the risk of sounding repetitive, faith and works are symbiotic and they make up a complete believer.

Abraham was counted righteous, or as James said was made perfect when he believed God. Abraham however was also made perfect when he took his son Isaac from home, and made the journey to the mountain God had instructed him to go to. In the first instance, wherein Abraham believed God, we see the inward faith of Abraham. In the second instance, wherein he took Isaac and was ready to sacrifice him, we see Abraham proving his inward faith before heaven and earth. It is worthwhile to ponder this difference, and realize that we must live outwardly what we have inwardly.

There must always be a balance between our faith, and its expression in good works. When faith is present in the life of a believer, God will speak to him time and again instructing him where to go, what he must do, who he must help, who he must comfort, who he must lift up, and who he must correct. All these things are the expression of our faith toward God, and our obedience toward His sovereign voice. When we obey, God continues to send us. He continues to instruct us, and He continues to task us with certain responsibilities. When we refuse to heed His voice, when we reject His stirring, when He speaks and we pretend as though we did not hear Him, He will send another to do what we ought to have done.

God is God. He does not beg, He commands! Regrettably many believers today have relegated God to being some shut in that is just happy to have the company whenever we decide to drop by. They have minimized the attributes of God to the point that He dares not ask anything of us, but offers us everything He has, just so we stay awhile longer. We dishonor God by minimizing Him and His attributes, by not seeing Him as He is...on the throne, full of glory and power. God is not the lowly bearded fellow who just wants to hug everybody we so readily envision Him to be. Though men attempt to shrink God down to their level, He remains God, forever possessing all authority and power over His creation.

He is God, and when His faith is poured into us, the outwardly manifestations of this faith must be evident in our lives. There is one last verse I want to touch upon, and I believe it clarifies once and for all the symbiosis between faith and works, as well as proves Biblically that they are, in fact, not mutually exclusive but are rather integral parts of a whole.

James 2:24, "You see then that man is justified by works, and not by faith only."

It is said that we are a product of our individual environment. Although I believe one can rise above their circumstances and their environment, I also believe that works of any kind must be a byproduct of our faith, wherein they have their root and their genesis. Men judge other men not by the words that come out of their mouths, but by their actions, their conduct, and even their reactions to certain events in their life. Someone can say they know how to tailor a suit, but if you give them the thread, the needle, and the necessary material and they can't follow through and prove that they know that which they claimed to know, then they are, by their own inability to perform the task, liars. It is true that first and foremost one learns the theory of tailoring, but if they never progress and practice what they learn, if they never practically apply the theory of their learning, then they can never call themselves a tailor.

It is the same with justification. Yes, we are justified by faith in Christ Jesus, but if we have come to Him and have not learned a new life, if we have not been transformed in our thinking, our desires, our way of life, and our outlook, then that faith is dead. First comes faith, then, due to the true and living faith that now resides in us, works must follow. First comes the tree, then, in order to know what sort of tree it is, whether good or bad, we must wait to see its fruit. Yes there are fruitless trees in the church, just as there are fruitless trees in an orchard, but those fruitless trees are soon cut down to make room for the trees that will bear fruit. As faithful servants of Christ, as followers of God, we must bear the fruit of our faith, and we must live this life with the full assurance that through faith in Jesus we will soon receive our eternal reward.

True faith, abiding faith, is one that is evident in an individual's life. True faith is not something that can be hidden, but rather something that is made manifest in all we do, and in all we say. It is who we are from the inside out, not temporarily but in perpetuity.

JAMES 2:18-20, "BUT SOMEONE WILL SAY, 'YOU HAVE FAITH, AND I HAVE WORKS.' SHOW ME YOUR FAITH WITHOUT YOUR WORKS, AND I WILL SHOW YOU MY FAITH BY MY WORKS. YOU BELIEVE THAT THERE IS ONE GOD. YOU DO WELL. EVEN THE DEMONS BELIEVE-AND TREMBLE. BUT DO YOU WANT TO KNOW, O FOOLISH MAN THAT FAITH WITHOUT WORKS IS DEAD?"

MATTHEW 3:13-15, "THEN JESUS CAME FROM GALILEE TO JOHN AT THE JORDAN TO BE BAPTISZED BY HIM. AND JOHN TRIED TO PREVENT HIM, SAYING, 'I HAVE NEED TO BE BAPTIZED BY YOU, AND ARE YOU COMING TO ME?' BUT JESUS ANSWERED AND SAID TO HIM, 'PERMIT IT TO BE SO NOW, FOR THUS IT IS FITTING FOR US TO FULFILL ALL RIGHTEOUSNESS.' THEN HE ALLOWED HIM."

CHAPTER FOUR
BAPTISMS

I know some might be thinking that I could have found a more exciting topic to expound upon, or write a book about, something that would get the blood pumping like end times prophecy, the book of Revelation, and as Paul said, 'this we will do if God permits.'

Prior to discussion of seals, bowls, plagues, and beasts, however, we must be certain that our foundation is well established, immovable, and unshakeable. There are some who make the tragic error of focusing on prophecy and the end times before their foundation is established, and since they have no foundation to speak of, they are swept away with the first storm that crosses their path.

Since I am, as my wife affectionately calls me, a prophecy geek, it would be far easier, and less time consuming for me to delve into the topic of end time prophecy, and write at length about it, but easier isn't always best, and I know it is far more important for believers to have a true and stable foundation, than to know what the future holds as pertains to the prophetic.

Is the prophetic irrelevant? By no means! Sometimes, however, we must do things in the order in which they were intended. Before we can graduate from college, we must first graduate high school, and before we can graduate high school we must first graduate elementary school and junior high. It is the way of things, and spiritually speaking there are many individuals today, walking about, believing they have a college degree, when they haven't yet successfully graduated elementary school. What we learn in elementary school is the foundation for our learning throughout our lives. We learn to read, to write, we learn addition, subtraction and multiplication, and these things aid us throughout our lives. As we grow and mature, we build on them. Spiritually speaking, the elementary principles of Christ, or the fundamental teachings are the tools by which, and with which we build upon.

I am a firm believer that whenever it comes to spiritual things, whenever it comes to supernatural things, it is paramount that we go directly to the source, directly to the Word, and see what God would teach us. There are many opinions floating about concerning spirituality, baptisms, the Holy Spirit, and anything else one might think of, but there is always only one truth and that is found in the Bible.

As such, you will not be reading my opinion on the doctrine of baptisms, but rather what the Word of God has to say about it. As followers of Christ, as worshippers of God, our duty is to submit to the authority of His Word, to submit to the authority of His will, and obey that which He commands. Too many have taken it upon themselves to interpret the will and mind of God. Too many have taken it upon themselves to twist the simple truth of God's Word toward their own nefarious ends, and we see the outcome of these distortions within the churches today, manifesting themselves by way of various deceptions and half-truths. The Bible is our instruction manual. It is the light by which we see the path upon which we must walk, and it is through the prism of this book that we will study and grow in grace, perceive and understand the importance of these fundamental teachings, and subsequently mature spiritually and deepen our relationship with God.

Although the Bible speaks of a handful of baptisms, from the baptism of Moses, to John's baptism, to the baptism of suffering, the baptism of the Holy Spirit, the baptism of fire, and the baptism into Christ for the remission of sins, within the context of this study on the doctrine of baptisms, we will be focusing on the three most relevant ones. As such, we will be discussing water baptism, or John's baptism, also known as the baptism of repentance, then move on to the baptism into Christ for the remission of sins, and finally the baptism of the Holy Spirit, the one baptism which has been woefully marginalized within the church for a very long time. If time and space permit, we will also discuss the baptism of suffering, or the baptism of fire which Christ spoke of, and of which he said He was to be baptized shortly before His crucifixion.

We will begin with the baptism of John, also known as the baptism of repentance, or more simply put, water baptism.

The word baptism itself comes from the Greek word 'baptizo', which in essence means to immerse or submerge. When John baptized with the baptism of repentance in the river Jordan, he immersed, or submerged those individuals who came seeking baptism.

Mark 1:4, "John came baptizing in the wilderness and preaching a baptism of repentance for the remission of sins."

Now some would ask, and rightly so, why I have separated the baptism of John, from the baptism into Christ for the remission of sins, and whether or not they were in fact one and the same. The short answer is that no, the baptism of John, and the baptism into Christ are not the same. John did not baptize in the name of Jesus... he simply baptized a baptism of repentance. The baptism of Christ, the baptism that Christ commanded His disciples to perform, was very specific, and when analyzed thoroughly we see the difference clearly delineated.

Matthew 28:19-20, "Go therefore and make disciples of all the nations, baptizing them in the name of the Father and of the Son and of the Holy Spirit, teaching them to observe all things that I have commanded you; and lo, I am with you always, even to the end of the age."

When Jesus commanded His disciples to go, He did not tell them to baptize everyone who showed up at the meetings. He did not tell them to baptize everyone they could talk into dunking in a river or a lake. The first command Jesus gave was to make disciples, and after these became disciples, they were to be baptized in the name of the Father and of the Son and of the Holy Spirit.

Dare I say there are many today who are being baptized, who are not Disciples of Christ. Dare I say there are many today who feel secure because they put on the white robe and got into the pool, but who were never discipled, who never knew the fullness of Christ, nor the things that Christ commands. Christ's first command was to make disciples. Once an individual was a disciple, then and only then were these newly made disciples to be baptized.

These are not semantics. They are glaring oversights made by many denominations today, because to disciple someone takes time, and effort, and wisdom, and knowledge of the Word of God. It is far easier to have someone raise a hand, say a prayer, dunk them in some tepid water, and call them saints requiring their tithe check as a sort of membership fee.

Now that we've cleared that up, let's return to the baptism of John or the baptism of repentance and see what we can learn of it, how it differs from the baptism of Christ, and what the Bible says about it.

In order to see the dramatic difference between the baptism of John, and the baptism of Christ, we need look no further than a certain Jew named Apollos, who was born at Alexandria. The Word tells us that Apollos was an eloquent man, and mighty in the Scriptures and as he journeyed, he came to Ephesus. This was by no means an ignorant man since the Bible also tells us he 'had been instructed in the way of the Lord, and that being fervent in spirit, he spoke and taught accurately the things of the Lord, though he knew only the baptism of John.'

Although Apollos had only known the baptism of John, he was still mighty in Scripture, instructed in the way of the Lord, fervent in spirit, and taught accurately the things of God.

Acts 18:26, "So he began to speak boldly in the synagogue. When Aquila and Priscilla heard him, they took him aside and explained to him the way of God more accurately."

So even though Apollos taught the things of God accurately, Aquila and Priscilla took him aside, and explained to him the way of God more accurately still. All Apollos had known was the baptism of John, until he met these two individuals who showed him more accurately the way of God.

Acts 18:1-6, "And it happened, while Apollos was at Corinth, that Paul, having passed through the upper

regions, came to Ephesus. And finding some disciples he said to them, 'Did you receive the Holy Spirit when you believed?' And they said to him, 'We have not so much as heard whether there is a Holy Spirit.' And he said to them, 'Into what then were you baptized?' So they said, 'Into John's baptism.' Then Paul said, 'John indeed baptized with a baptism of repentance, saying to the people that they should believe on Him who would come after him, that is, on Christ Jesus.' When they heard this, they were baptized in the name of the Lord Jesus. And when Paul had laid hands on them, the Holy Spirit came upon them, and they spoke with tongues and prophesied."

Within six verses, we see the three baptisms identified and enumerated individually. First we see the baptism of John, with which these men had already been baptized, we see the baptism of Christ, with which these men were baptized upon hearing of it, and finally we see the baptism of the Holy Spirit which these men received as Paul laid hands upon them, and they begin to speak in tongues and prophecy.

Once again – because it is very important – these are three distinct and separate baptisms.

So what were the requirements of receiving the baptism of John? Was it just showing up, standing in a line, saying you wanted to be baptized then proceeding to wade into the water? Surely John must have made it easy for people since so many went out to him that they might be baptized. Surely he could not have required anything of them because it would conflict with the modern adage of 'the less you require of people, the more people will flock to your cause!'

Matthew 3:1-6, "In those days John the Baptist came preaching in the wilderness of Judea, and saying, 'Repent, for the kingdom of heaven is at hand!' For this is he who was spoken of by the prophet Isaiah, saying: 'The voice of the one crying in the wilderness: prepare the way of the Lord, make His paths straight.' And John himself was clothed in camel's hair, with a leather belt around his waist; and his food was locusts and wild honey. Then Jerusalem, all Judea, and all the region around the Jordan went out to him and were baptized by him in the Jordan confessing their sins."

There were two non-negotiable requirements made of everyone that came to seek the baptism of John. First, they were to repent, and second, to confess their sins publicly. Only after they'd repented and confessed their sins, would John baptize those seeking his baptism. I realize this might seem outlandish to some in today's generation. How can such requirements be placed on individuals who simply desired to be baptized? These requirements were necessary so the baptism itself would be something more than taking a bath with one's clothes on. These requirements were necessary in order to place the individual squarely in front of the enormity of his sin and bring about repentance.

Even with these requirements, the Word tells us that Jerusalem, all Judea, and all the regions around the Jordan went out to John and were baptized by him in the Jordan.

Just as a side note, the remedy to dwindling church attendance and overall lack of interest toward the Christian faith is by no means the lowering of the bar or the lowering of the standards, but adherence to the truth of God's Word.

Many of the Pharisees and Sadducees of the time were also among those who came to be baptized by John. These were the power elites of the time, men with influence, and power, men with money and great authority among the people. Rather than be swayed by the men that stood before him, rather than attempt to accommodate them, John said to them, 'Brood of vipers! Who has warned you to flee from the wrath to come? Therefore bear fruits worthy of repentance, and do not think to say to yourselves, we have Abraham as our father.'

Absent repentance and absent fruit of repentance water baptism is a pointless exercise. The Pharisees and the Sadducees wanted the baptism of John, but without the requisite repentance and confession of sins. What they really wanted was an insurance policy against the wrath to come, not understanding the fact that absent true repentance, there could be no reconciliation with God... there could be no transformation or renewing of the mind.

Although John preached repentance, although Paul preached repentance, although Christ preached repentance as a mandatory step to being baptized, repentance has become taboo among many believers today, marginalized and sidestepped becoming a controversial topic among those who claim the name of Christ. Speak of anything else – even tell tall tales which have no basis in fact – but if you dare bring up repentance as a prerequisite to living a life in the fullness of Christ, if you dare bring up repentance as a mandatory experience in the life of every believer, then you will quickly be shunned, labeled a zealot, and banished by those who see themselves as progressive, all inclusive Christians.

Why have I returned to the topic of repentance again? Repentance and baptism are intertwined, and cannot be separated. One cannot occur and be of spiritual use unless the other is first and foremost done.

The baptism of John was a forerunner to the baptism of Christ, just as John the baptizer was a forerunner, or one who prepared the way of the Lord, for the Lord's arrival. We still discuss the baptism of John today, and it is still part of Christian tradition because not only did Jerusalem, all of Judea and all the region around the Jordan go out to him to be baptized, but there was one other who came to John that He might be baptized as well.

Matthew 3:13-15, "Then Jesus came from Galilee to John at the Jordan to be baptized by him. And John tried to prevent Him, saying, 'I have need to be baptized by You, and are You coming to me? But Jesus answered and said to him, 'Permit it to be so now, for thus it is fitting for us to fulfill all righteousness.' Then he allowed Him."

John recognized the authority and power of Christ, so when Jesus came to him to be baptized, John rightly surmised it was he who needed to be baptized by Jesus, and not the other way around. Was it mandatory for Jesus to be baptized with the baptism of John? No, it was not mandatory. He was the Son of God, He had no sins to confess, He had nothing to repent of, yet He was baptized with John's baptism that all righteousness might be fulfilled.

Jesus is our example. He is the prototype of that which we desire to be transformed into, and knowing this, Jesus went to be baptized. Christ was not baptized to be absolved of any sin, but so that when we come to believe, when we come to repent, when we come to confess our sins, we too might be baptized, not with John's baptism, but rather with His baptism.

The baptism of John, the baptism of law, the baptism of the old covenant and Old Testament, has been replaced by the baptism into Christ, the baptism of the new covenant and the baptism of grace. In essence the baptism of John became obsolete when the baton was passed, and the practice of baptism into Christ began.

Yes, the baptism of John differs from the baptism of Christ, for while the baptism of John was only one of repentance, the baptism of Christ adds to it, and completes it, including also the remission of sins.

Since both the baptism of John and the baptism of Christ for the remission of sins include the element of water, and of being submerged in water, before getting into the differences between the baptism of John and the baptism of Christ and before discussing baptism itself, I wanted to discuss the element of water. Throughout the Word of God it is conclusive and without equivocation that water is a religious symbol.

The Bible speaks of water as a symbol of creation, a symbol of destruction, and a symbol of purification. *2 Peter 3:5-6, "For this they willfully forget: that by the word of God the heavens were of old, and the earth standing out of the water, and in the water, by which the world that then existed perished, being flooded with water."*

Within the context of warning about the scoffers and those who would mock the Word of God, Peter reminds us what some willfully forget, that by the Word of God the earth stood out of the water, and in the water, and that the world which once existed, the world which perished, was flooded with water. Within this passage, as well as others, we see the element of water as a symbol of creation. Within this same passage we see the element of water as a symbol of destruction, as Peter reminds us of the great flood from which only Noah and his family escaped. Within the context of the parting of the red sea, and the subsequent destruction of Pharaoh and his armies, we also see water as a manifestation of God's judgment.

The last symbol to which the element of water is directly connected to in the Word is that of purification, and it can be traced as far back as the consecration of the priests in the book of Exodus. *Exodus 29:4, "And Aaron and his sons you shall bring to the door of the tabernacle of meeting, and you shall wash them with water."*

Numbers 19:7, "Then the priest shall wash his clothes, he shall bathe in water, and afterward he shall come into the camp;"

Ritual bathing in water and the fact that water is a symbol of purification can be traced back for millennia. The members of the tight knit community known as the Essenes at Qumran avoided any human contact whatsoever. They practiced daily ritual bathing, and practiced ablution or the ritual bathing of one's face and hands before every meal. In order to become a member of this community one had to go through two years of ritual bathing as prescribed by the Essenes at Qumran.

The reason I bring up Qumran and the Essenes, who were members of an ascetic Jewish sect in the first century before Christ, is because some consider that John adopted the practice of baptism from them, where it is believed that he was raised, but this is impossible for three reasons.

First, baptism is a singular, one time act, while the ablutions at Qumran ware repetitive in nature. Second, someone else administers baptism, while the ritualistic bathing at Qumran was self-induced. Third, while disciples of the Essenes at Qumran could only participate in the ritualistic bathing after two years, John baptized men the same day.

On one of those days, as John the baptizer was in the wilderness near the river Jordan preaching repentance and baptizing those who repented and confessed their sins, Jesus came from Galilee to be baptized by him.

John recognized the authority of Christ, the power of Christ, and the divinity of Christ. John knew that the baptism of Christ was far superior to his own, and in humility he said to Jesus that it was he who needed to be baptized by Him, and not the other way around.

We know that there was no sin in Christ. What Jesus was doing was instituting the means by which men ought to make a covenant with God and the means by which men would from that point forward dedicate their lives to the heavenly Father. Jesus was not being baptized with the baptism of repentance or confession of sins; He was instituting the new baptism, the baptism into Christ.

So why ought we to submerge individuals for baptism? For thus it is fitting. Why ought we not to baptize infants? Because an infant cannot repent, an infant does not know the difference between good and evil, but most importantly because thus it is fitting.

Jesus instituted true baptism by being baptized in the Jordan, and as such we must follow His example, for thus it is fitting for us to fulfill all righteousness. Through the act of baptism, Jesus demonstrated the fulfillment of the righteousness of God. He already was the righteousness of God, but by getting baptized, Jesus demonstrated it, and He showed it. Baptism is man's confession of having fulfilled the righteousness of God by faith; it is man's confession that in Christ and through Christ he has attained the righteousness of God; that he has been justified by faith.

Romans 5:1-2, "Therefore having been justified by faith, we have peace with God through our Lord Jesus Christ, through whom also we have access by faith into the grace in which we stand, and rejoice in the hope of the glory of God."

Jesus never simply told people what they must do. He first did it himself, and then said, 'you must do likewise'. First He loved, first He preached, first He healed, first He encouraged, first He rebuked, first He sacrificed, then after having first done these things, he taught us to do likewise. We must do as Jesus did, that we might become the image of Christ.

Matthew 3:16, "Then Jesus, when He had been baptized, came up immediately from the water; and behold, the heavens were opened to Him, and He saw the Spirit of God descending like a dove and alighting upon Him."

Having covered the generalities of baptism, I want to get into a few specifics, namely the requirements that one must fulfill in order to be baptized into Christ. Yes, there are requirements, there are conditions placed upon every man and woman who desire to make a covenant with God, and the first of these is something we spoke about at the beginning of this book, and that is repentance. Whenever we begin discussing the elementary principles of Christ, whenever we begin discussing the fundamental, or the foundational truths of the faith, repentance always seems to be intertwined within these teachings.

Acts 2:37-38, "Now when they had heard this, they were cut to the heart, and said to Peter and the rest of the apostles, 'men and brethren, what shall we do?' Then Peter said to them, 'repent, and let everyone of you be baptized in the name of Jesus Christ for the remission of sins; and you shall receive the gift of the Holy Spirit."

Peter had just finished preaching a resurrected Christ to a large number of individuals. He had just finished rebuking them, and they were cut to the heart at hearing his words. It was in this brokenness that these men asked Peter what they should do, and it is Peter's answer that I want to examine further.

Peter didn't tell them they needed to join a certain denomination, he didn't tell them they needed to contribute something to his work; Peter didn't tell them anything other than what John and Christ echoed throughout their ministries. Peter told the men who had been cut to the heart to repent!

The second requirement to being baptized into Christ is to believe. The individual seeking baptism must believe that Jesus is Lord that He is the Son of God, who hung on a cross, died, and rose again, that by His blood we are made clean, and by His stripes we are healed. In order for someone to be baptized, they must have faith in Christ, they must believe as Jesus told His disciples.

Mark 16:15-16, "And He said to them, "Go into all the world and preach the gospel to every creature. He who believes and is baptized will be saved; but he who does not believe will be condemned."

It is he who believes and is baptized that will be saved, not he who merely hears, not he that acknowledges Christ from a purely intellectual viewpoint, but he who believes in His divinity, and the imputation of His righteousness upon us.

The third requirement to being baptized into Christ is having a good conscience toward God. Before one can be baptized into Christ, before one can be immersed in the water, faith must have already taken place. Repentance, also must have already taken place, because in essence water baptism is the answer of a good conscience toward God. It is the testimony of the individual that these things have already occurred in his life and heart.

1 Peter 3:21-22, "There is also an antitype which now saves us, namely baptism (not the removal of the filth of the flesh, but the answer of a good conscience toward God), through the resurrection of Jesus Christ, who has gone into heaven and is at the right hand of God, angels and authorities and powers have been made subject to Him."

What Peter is saying is that, in and of itself, baptism does not remove the filth of the flesh, but rather the removal of the filth of the flesh must have already occurred before baptism. As such we are baptized as testimony of a good conscience toward God.

The last requirement is that one be a disciple of Christ. We have already discussed the fact that Jesus told His hearers to go and make disciples first, then baptize them in the name of the Father the Son and the Holy Spirit. One must first repent, believe, have a good conscience, and thereby become a disciple of Christ, and only then can they be baptized into Him.

The day one gets baptized is a day one will never forget. It has been well over twenty years since I was baptized and I still remember that day as clearly as when it first happened. I still remember my grandfather in his white robe, beckoning me into the water, I still remember being asked the questions whether I believed that Jesus is the only Son of God, that He died and rose again, that He is the way the truth of the life, and after confessing these things to be true being submerged into the chilly waters of the Pacific ocean.

I also remember having gone through much soul searching before asking to be baptized, the elders of the church asking if I was ready to make a lifelong commitment toward God, and if I had confessed what I felt I needed to confess before I took this step.

Baptism is not to be taken lightly. Baptism is not something one does simply to get it over with, but it is a covenant between man and God, an outwardly confession of an inner truth that one has established in their heart.

It is when we take the things of God lightly, when we look upon baptism as just a formality or a tradition that we must keep, that our hearts are insincere toward God, our motives and intent are impure, and all we end up doing is taking a bath with our clothes on. We must understand the true meaning of baptism into Christ, and the true meaning of being baptized from death into life, so we may learn to appreciate and place value on this once in a lifetime experience.

It is a glorious thing to know that once we are baptized, we have made a covenant with God, all our past is gone for good, and we are pure in His sight.

I touched on the topic of infant baptism if ever so briefly, and I know some might take issue with my stance on it, but after researching the Word thoroughly, and after spending much time in prayer concerning this topic, I felt I needed to discuss it in the light of Scripture.

There are two Scripture passages that adherents to infant baptism like to use as defense of this practice, one of them being the tenth chapter of Acts, which discusses Cornelius and his household as well as the sixteenth chapter of Acts, which details the interaction between the keeper of the prison, and Paul and Silas.

There are many who say that the word "household" includes infants and children not yet of age. From what the Bible tells us we can clearly see that this is not true, and if anything it is a distortion of God's holy Word.

Acts 10:1-2, "There was a certain man in Caesarea called Cornelius, a centurion of what was called the Italian Regiment, a devout man and one who feared God with all his household, who gave alms generously to the people, and prayed to God always."

So what we are told in the book of acts is that Cornelius was a devout man, and his entire household feared God. By these two verses, and the thirty-third verse of Acts chapter ten, wherein Cornelius says that 'they were all present before God, to hear all the things God commanded', we can deduce certain truths. First, all those of Cornelius's household were old enough to fear God, and second, they were old enough to be present that they might hear and perceive all the things that God commanded.

When the Word tells us that Cornelius's household was baptized, by the deductions we can readily make from Scripture we come to the understanding that all those who were of this household were of age, and able to discern. No babies were present! Babies can neither fear God nor desire to hear and perceive all the things that God commands...they are babies.

When Peter baptized those of Cornelius's household after they received the Holy Spirit, he baptized able-bodied men and women, and people of age who were able to discern.

The same can be said of the Philippian jailer, since those of his household were old enough to hear, receive, and believe, then be baptized. I realize it is a popular practice to baptize anyone and everyone, because the more baptisms we have on the rosters, the more conversions we can boast about, but Biblically speaking we can only baptize those who having heard the gospel, who having experienced repentance, who having believed, who having had the confession of a clean conscience, desire to make a covenant with God by baptism.

Why is baptism an important and integral part of our faith? Why is it listed among the fundamental teachings, or the elementary principles of Christ? Since the beginning of the primary church, baptism was practiced by those who believed. Beginning with the day of Pentecost, those who believed were baptized, but more importantly because Jesus Himself commanded that men be baptized in the name of the Father the Son and the Holy Spirit after having been made disciples.

Baptism is the symbol of death and resurrection. Paul tells us that by baptism we are buried together with Christ, dying to sin, dying to the world, and becoming alive in Him.

Romans 6:4-5, "Therefore we were buried with Him through baptism into death, that just as Christ was raised from the dead by the glory of the Father, even so we also should walk in newness of life. For if we have been united together in the likeness of His death, certainly we also shall be in the likeness of His resurrection."

Baptism into Christ is the symbol of our being united with Him; it is the confession of our faith in Christ. After we have been freed from the bonds of our old life we are given the power through Christ, and in Christ, to live a new life. As such, baptism makes our union with Christ visible, being the external manifestation of our having entered into the Body of Christ.

Contrary to the belief of some, baptism does not save. Although there are some passages within the Bible that if viewed superficially can cause one to come to this conclusion, the physical act of being submerged in water will not save one's soul. In all the Scriptures that would hint at baptism being the means to our salvation, we see the necessary ingredient plainly displayed, that ingredient being faith. We are continually exhorted that it is by faith we attain salvation, and not by the act of baptism.

Two things are prerequisites to baptism. Two things are required not by men, but by the Word of God, and there can be no exception or exemption for anyone. Those two things are repentance, and faith toward God. The repentance and faith I speak of are the selfsame repentance and faith toward God that Paul lists first in his enumeration of the elementary principles of Christ. Yes, baptism into Christ is a crucial component of our Christian walk, but baptism must be preceded by repentance and faith.

Lest we forget what Christ commanded His disciples, I want to reiterate:

Matthew 28:19 "Go therefore and make disciples of all nations, baptizing them in the name of the Father and of the Son and of the Holy Spirit."

Go therefore and make disciples, first! Make disciples of all nations! And only after you have made disciples, baptize them in the name of the Father and of the Son and of the Holy Spirit.

Another baptism we must discuss within the context of the doctrine of baptisms is the baptism of the Holy Spirit.

It seems in many a church, and many a denomination the Holy Spirit, the work of the Holy Spirit, and the baptism of the Holy Spirit, are as taboo a topic as the topic of repentance.

Whenever the topic of the baptism of the Holy Spirit is brought up in a church, there is invariably at least one individual who irate and flushed in the face stands up and says 'God doesn't do that anymore!'

When asked to prove the veracity of their claim Biblically however, they cannot, because contrary to the belief of some, when Jesus spoke about the Holy Spirit, He did not say that the Holy Spirit would be with us for a season or for a limited time. Rather, Jesus said that the Helper, the Holy Spirit would abide with us forever.

'Well if God is still doing it, if the Holy Spirit is still among us, and the baptism of the Holy Spirit is still available to the church, then why aren't we seeing it?'

Truth be known, there are parts in the world, and even churches in America that are seeing the outpouring the Holy Spirit. There are still those experiencing the gifts of the Holy Spirit, but to be blunt, God will not pour new wine into an old wineskin, and before we can hope to receive this baptism, we must first make certain that our vessels are clean, our wineskins are new, and that we are ready to receive that which God would gladly bestow upon us.

Let us begin – as the saying goes – at the beginning, and when discussing the advent, and the baptism of the Holy Spirit, there is no better place to begin than the book of Acts.

Acts 1:1-8, "The former account I made, O Theophilus, of all that Jesus began both to do and teach, until the day in which He was taken up, after He through the Holy Spirit had given commandments to the apostles whom He had chosen, to whom He also presented Himself alive after His suffering by many infallible proofs, being seen by them during forty days and speaking of the things pertaining to the kingdom of God. And being assembled together with them, He commanded them not to depart from Jerusalem, but to wait for the promise of the Father, 'which', He said, 'you have heard from Me; For John truly baptized with water, but you shall be baptized with the Holy Spirit not many days from now.' Therefore, when they had come together, they asked Him, saying, 'Lord will You at this time restore the kingdom to Israel?' And He said to them, "It is not for you to know times or seasons which the Father has put in His own authority. But you shall receive power when the Holy Spirit has come upon you; and you shall be witnesses to Me in Jerusalem, and in all Judea and Samaria, and to the end of the earth."

The book of Acts or the Acts of the Apostles begins where the gospel according to Luke leaves off. The same individual authors both. Luke was a doctor, an intelligent man with an eye for detail hired by a wealthy man named Theophilus to investigate Jesus, and come to a conclusion concerning His person. Whether Jesus truly was the Son of God, or the greatest of charlatans, Theophilus wanted to know, and he was willing to pay substantial sums to find out.

By hiring Luke and sending him to investigate Christ, we have two books of the Bible that would otherwise not have been, and throughout his investigative journey, from speaking to those who knew Christ, to traveling with Paul the Apostle, Luke came to the conclusion that indeed Jesus is the Son of God, He did die and rise again, and he confirms these truths in the first few lines of the book of Acts. Luke speaks of Christ presenting Himself alive after His sufferings, he speaks of infallible proofs, and of Jesus being seen speaking of things pertaining to the kingdom of God for forty days after His resurrection.

Within the first few verses of Acts, Luke also mentions the fact that Jesus commanded His disciples not to depart from Jerusalem, but to wait for the promise of the Father, which is the Holy Spirit, and with the baptism of the Holy Spirit they would also receive power.

The reason I bring up Luke, and the reason he is relevant, is because he began his investigation of Christ as an impartial third party. Luke had no vested interest in whether or not Jesus was who He claimed to be. He had simply been hired by a man to investigate the claims of the one known as Jesus of Nazareth, but his investigation led him to faith in Christ, to repentance and conversion. Christian history tells us that after preaching the gospel in Dalmatia, Gallia, Italy and Macedonia, Luke died as a martyr at the age of 74.

With that having been iterated, let us return to the discussion concerning the Holy Spirit, and the baptism thereof. To begin, because often times this unique experience is confused with other works of the Holy Spirit, I want to dispel certain misconceptions about the baptism of the Holy Spirit.

Contrary to popular belief within certain denominations, the baptism of the Holy Spirit is not the second work of grace. In fact this expression cannot be found anywhere in the Bible, but even so many continue to assert this fallacy as gospel truth. If we believe that grace manifests itself progressively through more than one work and that the baptism of the Holy Spirit is merely the second work of grace, why would we not believe that there is a third or a fourth work of grace as well?

What we can believe, because the Bible speaks of this, is that there is a continued intensification of grace within a believer. As Peter so eloquently states, we ought to continually grow in the grace and knowledge of our Lord and Savior Jesus Christ.

2 Peter 3:17-18, "You therefore, beloved, since you know these things beforehand, beware lest you also fall from your steadfastness, being led away with the error of the wicked; but grow in the grace and knowledge of the Lord and Savior Jesus Christ. To Him be the glory both now and forever. Amen."

There is another expression that is never found within the pages of Scripture, which still makes its rounds among many Christian groups when discussing the baptism of the Holy Spirit, and that is the assertion that the baptism of the Holy Spirit is the second blessing, or the second outpouring. Once again, I point to the fact that it is not found anywhere in the Bible, yet men continue to teach this strange doctrine.

The baptism of the Holy Spirit is not sanctification either. It is a separate work, a unique work, and although some say that sanctification is in fact what the baptism of the Holy Spirit is, Scripture itself contradicts this. Yes, sanctification is a work of the Holy Spirit, but it is by no means the baptism of the Holy Spirit.

Baptism with the Holy Spirit is also a separate work than that of being born again. It is a work that the same Holy Spirit of God performs, but it is a unique and distinctively different work than that of being born again, or regenerated. The baptism of the Holy Spirit completes the work of regeneration and sanctification that the Holy Spirit also performs in the hearts of those who have come to Christ.

On resurrection day, Jesus breathed on His disciples, and in John chapter 20, verse 22, the Word tells us that He said to them, 'Receive the Holy Spirit'. This was to show that regeneration and a new life was given to them. It was the selfsame resurrected Christ, who then tells His disciples that they must tarry in the city of Jerusalem until they would be endued with power from on high.

Luke 24:49, "Behold, I send the Promise of My Father upon you; but tarry in the city of Jerusalem until you are endued with power from on high."

So why is this important? What does it mean, and why is it relevant to our discussion of the baptism of the Holy Spirit?

It is important because it clearly shows that the baptism of the Holy Spirit was a completely different experience for the Disciples of Christ than that of being born again. First, Christ breathed on His disciples and said, 'receive the Holy Spirit' but then He tells His disciples to remain in Jerusalem until they receive the power of the Holy Spirit.

I know it may irk a certain segment of Christendom, but it is Biblically proven that conversion or regeneration, being born again, and the baptism of the Holy Spirit, or the infilling with power from on high as Jesus called it, are two distinct and unique experiences.

Another thing that the baptism of the Holy Spirit is not is conversion. I know, I know, certain scholars and theologians keeps saying that conversion and receiving the baptism of the Holy Spirit are synonymous, that they are one and the same thing, but once again we return to the Word of God, and let it have the final say.

The aforementioned Word of God, the Bible offers us clear examples that prove beyond a shadow of doubt that conversion and the baptism of the Holy Spirit are two distinct, unique, and different experiences.

The first example of conversion and the baptism of the Holy Spirit being two unique, distinct, and different experiences can be found in the eighth chapter of Acts. Although the Samaritans were converted through the preaching of Phillip, they received the baptism of the Holy Spirit a few days later through the ministry of Peter and John.

Although the Samaritans believed Philip as he preached the things concerning the kingdom of God and the name of Jesus Christ, although both men and women were baptized, it was only later that they received the baptism of the Holy Spirit.

Acts 8:14-17, "Now when the apostles who were at Jerusalem heard that Samaria had received the word of God, they sent Peter and John to them, who, when they had come down, prayed for them that they might receive the Holy Spirit. For as yet He had fallen upon none of them. They had only been baptized in the name of the Lord Jesus. Then they laid hands on them, and they received the Holy Spirit."

Just to make this point as clearly as possible, although they had been converted, although they had been baptized in the name of the Lord Jesus, they had as yet not received the Holy Spirit. Only After Peter and John laid hands on them, did they receive the Holy Spirit! These were individuals who had been converted, who believed, who had repented, who had even been baptized, yet the apostles laid hands on them that they might receive the Holy Spirit.

If the Holy Spirit is received at conversion as some continue to assert, then why pray tell did Peter and John pray over these individuals, and how is it that they actually received something more? How is it that they received the Holy Spirit if they already had the Holy Spirit?

The second example I want to highlight is that of Paul's conversion on the road to Damascus. There exists no doubt regarding Paul's conversion on the road to Damascus. The question that remains to be asked is: did he also receive the Holy Spirit upon his conversion?

Biblical answer: no, he did not. Paul received the Holy Spirit three days later, through the ministry of Ananias.

Acts 9:17, "And Ananias went his way and entered the house; and laying his hands on him he said, 'Brother Saul, the Lord Jesus, who appeared to you on the road as you came, has sent me that you may receive your sight and be filled with the Holy Spirit."

I do hope that we've established this truth as self-evident by way of Scripture, namely, that conversion and the baptism of the Holy Spirit are not one and the same, but rather two very different experiences.

Another misconception we must dispel is that the baptism of the Holy Spirit is sanctification. The baptism of the Holy Spirit is not sanctification. Yes, sanctification is a work of the Holy Spirit, but the baptism of the Holy Spirit and sanctification are two individual works.

Sanctification is a manifestation of the grace of God, which presents itself in two different ways. First, is instant sanctification due to the Word of God, and second, is progressive sanctification, a process, by which an individual is sanctified.

Lest you label me a heretic, both of these means of sanctification are found in the Word, and I want to go through a couple of the Bible passages just so there is no doubt on your part.

It is none other than Jesus who speaks of instant sanctification, as He says the following to His disciples in John 15:3, *"You are already clean because of the word which I have spoken to you."*

Jesus did not say they were in the process of becoming clean, or that they would become clean, but rather they were already clean because of the Word that He had spoken to them.

There are also Scriptures in the Bible that support progressive sanctification, and I will quickly go through a few just to establish this truth in your heart.

1 Thessalonians 5:23-24, "Now may the God of peace Himself sanctify you completely; and may our whole spirit, soul, and body be preserved blameless at the coming of our Lord Jesus Christ. He who calls you is faithful, who also will do it."

Hebrews 6:1, "Therefore, leaving the discussion of the elementary principles of Christ, let us go on to perfection."

In both Thessalonians, and Hebrews, Paul speaks of a progressive sanctification. Whether going on to perfection, or being sanctified completely, both of these terms signify a work in progress, an ongoing process that had not as yet been completed. Whether through instant sanctification, or progressive sanctification, it is God's choosing how we will be sanctified. The point of it all is that sanctification, and the baptism of the Holy Spirit, are not one and the same work.

Yet another misconception about the baptism of the Holy Spirit is that it is somehow a reward. I have heard it often, and from different men over the years that the baptism of the Holy Spirit is a reward for the years of service one puts in as a disciple of Christ, and it represents the pinnacle of the Christian experience. Some also share the false misconception that the baptism of the Holy Spirit somehow marks an individual as having achieved a superior state of spirituality.

Both of these opinions are false, untrue, and have no basis in Scripture. The Word tells us the baptism of the Holy Spirit is the promise of the Father, and Peter, while speaking to a large crowd that had assembled before him, states that after being baptized in water, they would receive the gift of the Holy Spirit.

Acts 2:38, "Then Peter said to them, 'repent, and let everyone of you be baptized in the name of Jesus Christ for the remission of sins; and you shall receive the gift of the Holy Spirit."

Peter didn't say that they would have to wait for years, he did not say they would have to prove themselves first, he told those who had been cut to the heart at hearing his words, that they must repent, be baptized in the name of Jesus Christ for the remission of sins, and they would receive the gift of the Holy Spirit.

Within this same passage of Scripture, we also see that the outpouring of the Holy Spirit, the baptism of the Holy Spirit was not exclusive to the day of Pentecost as some continue to affirm.

Acts 2:39, "For the promise is to you and to your children and to all who are afar off, as many as the Lord our God will call."

Peter is saying that the gift of the Holy Spirit, was not exclusive to that day or that generation, but even to their children, and all who were afar off, meaning those many years from that present time, as many as the Lord God will call. Just because certain individuals educated beyond their intelligence still continue to deny the actuality of the baptism of the Holy Spirit, and the work of the Holy Spirit as being for today, does not make it so. It never ceases to astound me how some choose this topic as their last stand, denying the presence and power of the Holy Spirit with such vehemence as to shock even the godless. Just as the sacrifice of Christ Jesus is eternal, able to restore, and reconcile men unto God from generation to generation, the baptism of the Holy Spirit is likewise a perpetual experience.

There is one more misconception I would like to clear up, the affirmation that the baptism of the Holy Spirit is a collective experience. Once again, Biblically speaking, the baptism of the Holy Spirit is not a collective experience but an individual one.

Although there were one hundred and twenty people in the upper room awaiting the promise, although they experienced the baptism of the Holy Spirit at the same time, the tongues as of fire appeared and sat upon each of them individually.

Acts 2:4-5, "Then there appeared to them divided tongues, as of fire, and one sat upon each of them. And they were all filled with the Holy Spirit and began to speak with other tongues as the Spirit gave them utterance."

The baptism of the Holy Spirit is a personal and intimate experience. It is not shared collectively but rather God searches the individual heart, and pours out His Holy Spirit individually.

Since we've discussed the misconceptions concerning the baptism of the Holy Spirit, it would be wise to begin discussing what the Bible tells us about the Holy Spirit and the baptism thereof.

I want to begin by answering a simple yet profound question: What is the baptism of the Holy Spirit?

Simply put, the baptism of the Holy Spirit is a unique experience, initiated by the triune God, and realized supernaturally. It is the promise of the Father, and a gift to those who have come to repentance, and received Christ as Lord and Savior.

Since I promised at the beginning of this book that we will explore these elementary principles of Christ through the prism of God's Word and I strive to be a man of my word, we will go through a few Scriptures that bear out the truth of what the baptism of the Holy Spirit is. How do we know that the triune God initiates the baptism of the Holy Spirit? Simple answer: because Jesus told us.

John 16:7, "Nevertheless I tell you the truth. It is to your advantage that I go away; for if I do not go away, the Helper will not come to you; but if I depart, I will send Him to you."

It must have been quite a sight to see the Disciples of Christ react to what Jesus said in this passage. How could it be to their advantage that Jesus go away? How could it possibly be to their advantage that their Lord, the one whom they had forsaken everything to follow, would depart from them? Because Jesus promised He would not leave them as orphans, but He would send the Holy Spirit, the Helper, who would give them power to go and preach the gospel to all nations.

We know that the Holy Spirit is a gift, because Peter said as much while he was speaking to the crowd that had been cut to the heart, but also because of what he says in another passage in the book of Acts.

Acts 5:32, "And we are His witnesses to these things, and so also is the Holy Spirit whom God has given to those who obey Him."

There are many other Scriptures we could go through, but just by these two Scriptures alone we can glean that the baptism of the Holy Spirit is not merited, it is not a reward, and it is not a result of our labors or of our sacrifices. The baptism of the Holy Spirit is a gift of the grace of God, and this is how we ought to perceive it.

Now that we've established what the baptism of the Holy Spirit is, i.e. a gift of God, and a unique experience for believers, I want to spend some time and discover the purpose of it, and the reason it is necessary for us as believers today. In other words, what is it good for, and why should you have it?

It is no exaggeration when I say that the baptism of the Holy Spirit is important in every aspect of our walk of faith, neither is it hyperbole. Just so we get an idea of the importance of the Holy Spirit in our Christian walk, I want to go through some of the benefits of this gift, not from my point of view, but from what the Word of God says about it.

First, the Holy Spirit gives us strength; He gives us power in our service toward God, and aids us in ministering to those around us.

Luke 4:18-19, "The Spirit of the Lord is upon Me, because He has anointed Me to preach the gospel to the poor, He has sent Me to heal the brokenhearted, to preach deliverance to the captives, and recovery of sight to the blind. To set at liberty those who are oppressed, to preach the acceptable year of the Lord."

These were not the words of any mere man, but the words of Christ Jesus. What we must understand is that the life and ministry of Christ were dominated by this power. It was because the Spirit of the Lord was upon Him that He was able to heal, preach deliverance, set free, and preach the gospel.

Jesus also promised his Disciples something truly remarkable once they received this power and this gift.

John 14:12, "Most assuredly, I say to you, he who believes in Me, the works that I do he will do also; and greater works than these he will do, because I go to My Father."

Did this promise ever come to pass? Did the Disciples of Christ do the works He did? Read the Acts of the Apostles, and you will see miracle after miracle, healing after healing, thousands upon thousands believing in Jesus and being baptized both in water and the Holy Spirit. So yes, this promise began its fulfillment on the day of Pentecost.

The gift of the Holy Spirit also elevates our fellowship with God to the level of a personal experience, not something that we hear about from other sources, or second hand retellings of other men's experiences.

When Peter recounts His ministry to the gentiles, in Acts Chapter 11, he says something very telling.

Acts 11:15, "And as I began to speak, the Holy Spirit fell upon them, as upon us at the beginning.

Romans 8:26, "Likewise the Spirit also helps in our weaknesses. For we do not know what we should pray for as we ought, but the Spirit Himself makes intercession for us with groaning which cannot be uttered."

Do we understand the full weight of this verse? Are we beginning to see how necessary the Holy Spirit is in the life of a believer? The Spirit Himself makes intercession for us, even when we do not know what we should pray for, as we ought. This is amazing, and this passage continues and tells us that He who searches the heart knows what the mind of the Spirit is, because He makes intercession for the saints according to the will of God.

Seeing how precious a gift the baptism of the Holy Spirit is, seeing how necessary it is for us as believers, the next question that we must ask is who was it intended for?

Was the baptism of the Holy Spirit only for those who lived in apostolic times? Was the baptism of the Holy Spirit intended only for missionaries, evangelists and pastors? Was it intended only for the privileged class, or for mature Christians?

The answer to all these questions is a resounding no. No, it was not intended only for those who lived in apostolic times since Peter testified that this gift was for those who heard him, for their children, and for those afar off; No, the baptism of the Holy Spirit is not just for missionaries, evangelists and pastors since every member in the body of Christ is equally important, and all of us, to the last, must war against the enemy; No, the baptism of the Holy Spirit was not intended only for the privileged class, or for mature Christians, because God is not a respecter of persons, and He does not subscribe to the idea of nepotism.

The baptism of the Holy Spirit, the gift of the Holy Spirit is for all those who believe!

John 7:38-39, "He who believes in Me, as the Scripture has said, out of his heart will flow rivers of living water. But this He spoke concerning the Spirit, whom those believing in Him would receive; for the Holy Spirit was not yet given, because Jesus was not yet glorified."

Who spoke these words? Jesus! What did he promise to those who believe in Him? That out of their hearts will flow rivers of living water. Kind of obscure if the Bible would not have explained further, but it does. It tells us that this He spoke concerning the Spirit whom those believing in Him would receive, for the Holy Spirit was not yet given.

Although we can go further, and point out where the primary church believed that the Holy Spirit was for all believers, and where Peter testifies the same thing, I think we can take the words of Jesus as truth, as fact, as unshakable, and move on to the next question, which I must warn you is a tough one.

If we have Biblically established that the baptism of the Holy Spirit is still for today, if we have Biblically established that it is a necessary component in the life of every believer, why is it that so many deny this baptism, and some vehemently so?

To be frank, many deny the baptism of the Holy Spirit because it comes with conditions that God requires of us in order to receive it. Whether due to their doctrinal upbringing or outright indifference, an alarming number of self-professing Christians are simply unwilling to meet God's requirements.

What are God's requirements? Foremost is repentance. We return to Peter and the large crowd he was speaking to and the first requirement that he laid out; the first thing he told them they must do is repent.

The second requirement that God has for receiving the gift of the Holy Spirit is that we be born again.

Holy Spirit can be received Biblically, it is only fair that we discuss the obstacles that stand in the way of receiving this gift.

For many today, the greatest obstacle standing in the way of receiving the baptism of the Holy Spirit is the preconceived notions we harbor and cling to. Jesus did not explain how they would receive the Holy Spirit to His disciples, and His disciples did not ask. They waited in Jerusalem as commanded, until the promise descended. Some have already made up their mind concerning the baptism of the Holy Spirit, and they will not be swayed. Though one might try to Biblically prove out the actuality of this gift, their preconceived beliefs keep them from receiving it.

The second obstacle standing in the way of receiving the baptism of the Holy Spirit is that of discouragement. Man has a tendency to grow discouraged if his expectations are not met, and discouragement can come about if the experience of the baptism of the Holy Spirit is delayed. Yes, sometimes God tests our patience, and all we can do is persevere and wait on the Lord until He pours out His blessing. We cannot dictate terms to God. We are servants thus we serve, and wait on Him knowing all things will come to pass in His time.

The third obstacle is doubt. Many professing Christians today doubt the very existence of this promise, as well as the possibility of coming into possession of it. Listed in the top tier of obstacles that stand in the way of receiving the baptism of the Holy Spirit is also lack of consecration, as well as refusal to confess one's sin. If the baptism of the Holy Spirit is seen as merely an alternative or an option, then problems will surely arise. The baptism of the Holy Spirit must be seen as a necessity, and this is why a complete and total dedication as well as a hunger and desire for this baptism are paramount.

Since it is an often misunderstood component, I want to discuss the evidence and the resulting effects of the baptism of the Holy Spirit. The baptism of the Holy Spirit is comprised of two elements. First is the receiving of a special power from the Holy Spirit, and second is the physical initial sign of the presence of this baptism that is manifested by speaking in tongues.

Yes, speaking in tongues is Biblical, and it is the immediate evidence of having received the baptism of the Holy Spirit. Speaking in tongues is a supernatural manifestation of the Holy Spirit, through which the believer speaks in another tongue, a tongue that he has not studied or learned. Tongues can either be known languages of the earth, but they can also be unknown tongues.

Speaking in tongues can be received as a sign that one has received the baptism of the Holy Spirit, or as a gift, meaning one of the nine gifts of the Holy Spirit. When speaking in tongues is the sign that one has received the baptism of the Holy Spirit, the spirit of the believer and the Holy Spirit unite and praise and verbally prophesy. Tongues are not provoked by the mind of man, but they work in concert with our mental faculties.

1 Corinthians 13:14, "What is the result then? I will pray with the spirit, and I will also pray with the understanding. I will sing with the spirit, and I will also sing with the understanding."

Nowhere in Scripture does it say that the Holy Spirit is speaking in tongues but that we speak in tongues. Paul declares as such when he says, 'for if I pray in another tongue, my spirit prays'.

The baptism of the Holy Spirit took place in Jerusalem, Samaria, Damascus, Caesarea, and Ephesus as the book of Acts tells us. In three of the five cases, the sign of this experience was clearly defined. Although there exists a variety in the way we receive the baptism of the Holy Spirit, whether by prayer, instantaneously or by laying on of hands, speaking in tongues was and is an integral part of it in every case. The first, as well as the last mention of the baptism of the Holy Spirit in the book of Acts, also includes the mention speaking in tongues.

The Church was born on resurrection day when Christ breathed on His disciples and said, 'take Holy Spirit', and it was equipped with power on the day of Pentecost so it might preach the gospel of the kingdom of God with authority. The baptism of the Holy Spirit is what equips the saints to walk the narrow path of faith, and absent the baptism of the Holy Spirit we are ill equipped to fight the battles that we know we must fight along the way.

Speaking in tongues is not a power, but it is the proof that there is a power in us. Tongues are the proof that we have received the baptism of the Holy Spirit, but once we have received it we must continue to grow in the grace and gifts of God. For many, speaking in tongues is a purpose in and of itself. However, it ought not to be so. There is more to the baptism of the Holy Spirit than the initial evidence of speaking in tongues, and once we understand the power and authority that comes with this anointing we will be able to perform great exploits for the Kingdom.

I realize there are still many aspects of the baptism of the Holy Spirit that I did not cover, but the purpose of this book is to understand the elementary principles of Christ. The person of the Holy Spirit is a deep and wide topic, far too complex to cover in this book alongside the other fundamentals of the faith.

My prayer is that you now have a general knowledge of the baptism of the Holy Spirit, its benefits, its necessity, its present availability, and the fact that Jesus promised it to all those who believe, who humble themselves in repentance, and who cry out to Him in faith.

AS WITH ALL THINGS WHICH GOD INSTRUCTS US TO DO IN HIS WORD, THERE IS A WELL-DEFINED PURPOSE FOR THE LAYING ON OF HANDS, ONE THAT WE MUST UNDERSTAND IN ORDER TO APPRECIATE THIS DOCTRINE EVEN THOUGH IT HAS BEEN RELEGATED TO THE DUSTBIN OF FORGOTTEN CHURCH HISTORY FOR MANY DECADES NOW.

CHAPTER FIVE
THE LAYING ON OF HANDS

Since the author of Hebrews mentions laying on of hands as an elementary principle of Christ, one can't help but wonder what is so important about this solemn act, and why it ought to continue being practiced in the church today. In this chapter I will discuss the definition, the purpose, and the practice of laying on of hands both in the Old Testament as well as the New Testament.

Why would Paul list the laying on of hands as one of the elementary principles of Christ? Why is it relevant? Why would it be important enough to share the same stage as the doctrine of baptism, repentance, faith toward God, the resurrection of the dead, and the doctrine of eternal judgment?

Because dear friend, the elementary principle of the laying on of hands is far deeper than one might believe at first glance, and there is much this practice entails.

So why is the doctrine of the laying on of hands so important? Why is it relevant enough that Paul felt compelled to include it among the elementary principles of Christ? In short, the teaching, or the doctrine of the laying on of hands is important for the body of Christ, because it assures the continuity of the Church. In other words, the practice of the laying on of hands assures the continuity of spiritual life from one generation to the next.

The lack of teaching coupled with the marginalizing and avoidance of this doctrine both from a theological viewpoint as well as a practical one, has caused it to be only sparingly represented in the life of what we would call the contemporary church.

As with all things which God instructs us to do in His Word, there is a well-defined purpose for the laying on of hands, one that we must understand in order to appreciate this doctrine even though it has been relegated to the dustbin of forgotten church history for many decades now.

Laying on of hands is a practice which the primary church embraced from the olden days, through which God transfers – through a chosen vessel – a power of the Holy Spirit meant to bring blessing, healing, strength and the manifestation of certain gifts among which we can also count the baptism of the Holy Spirit.

The elemental purpose of this practice is that of identifying. The individual laying hands on another, identifies the future growth, future blessing, future fellowship or the future ministry of the person he is laying hands upon. It is not a practice that we ought to take lightly or do hastily, but rather one which is reserved only for when the Spirit of God stirs us to do it, and only for when we know it is in fact God who compelled us to lay hands on someone. Laying hands on others hastily is dangerous, because a connection is established between the two individuals, and if it is done hastily and not in a sanctified manner there can be grievous consequences.

1 Timothy 6:22, "Do not lay hands on anyone hastily, nor share in other people's sins. Keep yourself pure."

What is the purpose of laying on of hands, and what does it actually do?

The best way I can explain it, is that the laying on of hands acts as a conduit that allows the transfer of power from God, through one individual and into another. Before anyone gets too excited, there is nothing mystical about the laying on of hands. It is something natural and a practice embraced by the early church. Mothers lay hands on their children's foreheads to see if they are warm, and men greet each other by laying their hand on one another's shoulder. All these actions are natural, but what the Holy Spirit does is He takes this natural action and adds a spiritual component to it.

When we lay hands on others compelled by God, there are certain things that we can transfer or transmit to those we are laying hands upon.

By the laying on of hands we can transfer or transmit blessing. We see this in the Old Testament, beginning with Joseph seeing his father lay his right hand on the head of Ephraim and blessing him.

By the laying on of hands we can also transfer or transmit wisdom.

Deuteronomy 34:9, "Now Joshua the son of Nun was full of the spirit of wisdom, for Moses had laid his hands on him; so the children of Israel heeded him, and did as the Lord had commanded Moses."

The Word is very clear that Joshua the son of Nun was full of the spirit of wisdom because Moses had laid his hands on him. By laying hands on Joshua, Moses transferred the spirit of wisdom to him.

By the laying on of hands we can also transfer, or transmit the Holy Spirit. Before citing Biblical precedent, I must say that the practice of attempting to transfer the Holy Spirit by the laying on of hands has been widely abused in today's modern church. We see this most often with men standing in lines, having their foreheads touched and believing they received the Spirit. Just because something is abused in certain churches or denominations does not invalidate it, nor does it nullify the veracity of it. Yes, the Apostles laid hands on men that they might receive the Holy Spirit. It is a Biblical reality that we cannot deny or pretend does not exist.

When Peter and John came to the city of Samaria inquiring if those who had been baptized had received the Holy Spirit, upon hearing that they had not the Word tells us in Acts 8:17 that they laid hands on them, and they received the Holy Spirit. So yes, it is Scriptural, and Biblical, and nowhere in the Bible are we told that this practice somehow ended or was nullified by God.

By the laying on of hands we can also transfer, or transmit authority. When the Apostles of Christ picked seven men of good reputation, full of the Holy Spirit, and wisdom to watch over the daily distribution of food to the widows, they were brought before the apostles, and when they had prayed, they laid hands on them.

After laying hands on them these men went out preaching the Word, and did great signs and wonders among the people.

Spiritual gifts can also be transferred or transmitted by the laying on of hands. In his second letter to Timothy, Paul reminds him to stir up the gift of God that was in him by the laying on of his hands.

2 Timothy 1:6, "Therefore I remind you to stir up the gift of God which is in you through the laying on of my hands."

That is pretty self-explanatory. Once again, my purpose in writing this book is to see what the Word of God says concerning these elementary principles of Christ, these fundamental doctrines of the faith, and not what some denomination or some individual has to say about them. When we go to the Word of God, we know that the truth we receive is established in God.

Although there are countless instances in the Old Testament wherein the laying on of hands was incorporated, whether for blessing, for ordination, or for transferring the sin of the individual to the animal the Levites were about to sacrifice if only symbolically so, I also want to establish the use of laying on of hands in the New Testament.

While bestowing blessings was the primary use of laying on of hands in the Old Testament, in the New Testament, Jesus introduced the practice to be used for healing. Jesus often laid hands on the sick in His ministry, and this He did in two ways. He laid hands on the sick directly, but also indirectly, or by simply touching someone.

There are countless examples of Jesus laying hands on the sick and restoring them throughout the four gospels, but there are also examples wherein Jesus simply touched someone's blind eyes, or someone's deaf ears, and they were healed. The Apostles also utilized the laying on of hands when praying for the sick that they might be healed. The Bible reasserts this truth by telling us in Acts 5:12, that *'through the hands of the Apostles many signs and wonders were done.'*

So who can lay hands on others? If it is one of the elementary principles of Christ, if it is something that the Word of God encourages us to do, whether for healing, blessing, power, or authority, the question that remains to be asked is who exactly is Biblically allowed to lay hands on others?

If we study the Bible with diligence, within its pages we see who it was that laid hands on others. Just as throughout the universe there is an established order to things, God has an established order as well. It always amazes me when I go into a church and I see everyone laying hands on everyone else, from little children to fully-grown adults, as though it was something ordinary...as though it was something irrelevant.

'Just stretch out your hand and lay it on the person next to you.'

Sounds easy enough, but whom does the Bible say laid hands on others? Whom does the Bible identify as those commissioned to lay hands on the sick, on the possessed, on those needing strength and the power of God?

There are three categories of individuals that the Bible specifies laid hands on others. The first category the Bible speaks of, as laying hands on others, were the Apostles. Once again we return to the seven men who were chosen to serve tables, and we see that they were brought before the Apostles who after praying laid hands on them. It was not the entire congregation, but the Apostles who laid hands on these men. The second and third categories of individuals who the Bible speaks of as having laid hands on others are prophets, followed by teachers.

Acts 13:1-3, "Now in the church that was at Antioch there were certain prophets and teachers: Barnabas, Simeon who was called Niger, Lucius of Cyrene, Manaen who had been brought up with Herod the tetrarch, and Saul. As they ministered to the Lord and fasted, the Holy Spirit said, 'now separate to Me Barnabas and Saul for the work to which I have called them.' Then, having fasted and prayed, and laid hands on them, they sent them away."

It was these prophets and teachers who the Bible speaks of that laid hands on Saul and Barnabas for the work which God had called them to. Then, they were sent away to go and pursue the ministry to which God had called them. Now the Bible tells us there was a church at Antioch, yet only these prophets and teachers laid hands on Barnabas and Saul.

Why didn't everybody just come up and lay hands on them? Because throughout the Bible we can clearly see that those who laid hands on others were men with the authority of God, full of the Holy Spirit, and recognized by the early church. In every case – with the exception of healing – the elders were those who laid hands on individuals. Due to the serious nature of the things laying on of hands entails, immature individuals are not allowed to participate in it.

The last category of individuals who the Bible speaks of as having laid hands on others, are the elders. In his first letter to Timothy, Paul mentions the presbytery, or the elders of the church, and the fact that they had laid hands on him.

1 Timothy 4:14, "Do not neglect the gift that is in you, which was given to you by prophecy with the laying on of hands of the presbytery."

Having discussed who it is the Bible says can lay hands on others, I want to discuss if only briefly, the conditions one must meet in order for the laying on of hands to have an effect.

Yes, there are conditions, and even though today's church has chosen to ignore the word 'if' in the Bible, God is still God, His Word is still His Word, and when God says 'if' you do a certain thing then I will likewise do a certain thing, He means what He says.

The first condition an individual must meet in order for the laying on of hands to have an effect is they must have faith in God. Absent faith in God, we can have elders, and prophets, teachers and apostles lay hands on us until kingdom come with no effect and no visible demonstration of any power.

As Jesus stood before the tomb of Lazarus who had been dead for four days, as Mary and Martha stood beside Him pleading with Him not to take away the stone from the tomb since there would be a stench, Jesus said something to Martha that we must all take to heart.

John 11:40, "Jesus said to her, 'did I not tell you that if you believe you would see the glory of God?"

When we lay hands on an individual, be it for healing, for restoration or for the power of God, they must believe. If we believe, we too will see the glory of God. If we believe we too will see the miracles of God. Absent belief, absent faith, we will see absolutely nothing, because faith stirs the heart of God and puts the plan of God into action.

John 14:12, "Most assuredly, I say to you, he who believes in Me, the works that I do he will do also; and greater works than these he will do, because I go to my Father."

The second condition we must meet in order for the laying on of hands to have an effect is to fast and to pray. Yes, a prayer life, and a life of fasting are essential ingredients in ensuring that when we, by the unction of the Holy Spirit lay hands on someone, they will be healed, restored, receive power, and have authority.

There was a revelatory exchange between Christ and His disciples when a man who had an epileptic son came to Jesus and asked for healing on his behalf. During his dialogue with Christ, the man also informed Him of having first gone to His disciples, but they were unable to cure him. After rebuking the demon and after the demon had come out of him, the child was cured from that very hour, but the Disciples of Christ were perplexed as to why they could not do the same thing sometime earlier. Why was it, they inquired, that they could not cast out the demon?

Matthew 17:20-21, "So Jesus said to them, 'Because of your unbelief; for assuredly, I say to you, if you have faith as a mustard seed, you will say to this mountain, 'move from here to there,' and it will move; and nothing will be impossible for you. However, this kind does not go out except by prayer and fasting."

We tend to forget that although Jesus was the Christ, the Son of God, He spent more time in prayer than any of His disciples. It is often that we find Jesus alone, withdrawn, by Himself praying to the Father for strength and for guidance. If Jesus had a prayer life, then as His disciples we must likewise have a healthy and consistent prayer life. As Jesus said, there are certain evils; there are certain demons that do not go out except by fasting and prayer. He didn't say except by the laying on of hands, but fasting and prayer, which equip you so when you do go and prayerfully lay hands on someone, God answers the prayer.

For those who are receiving prayer, for those who are having hands laid on them there is also a condition that they must meet. It is important we discuss it, because tragically, it is a practice that has fallen out of favor with much of today's church.

The practice I speak of is that of confessing one's sin before they receive prayer.

James 5:14-16, "Is anyone among you sick? Let him call for the elders of the church, and let them pray over him, anointing him with oil in the name of the Lord. And the prayer of faith will save the sick, and the Lord will raise him up. And if he has committed sins, he will be forgiven. Confess your trespasses to one another, and pray for one another, that you may be healed. The effective fervent prayer of a righteous man avails much."

I realize in our politically correct, non-confrontational, non-offensive society it might be difficult to speak to someone about confessing his or her sins. I realize it may get a bit awkward, but it must be done because the Bible says it must be done. 'Confess your trespasses, and pray for one another, that you may be healed.' What this verse is saying is that in order to be healed, we must do these two things: confess and pray.

The laying on of hands is always accompanied by prayer, showing us that the gifts of grace and of healing are from God, and not from the act of one individual laying his hands on another. It is the Lord that heals. It is the Lord that saves. It is the Lord that forgives. We are vessels; we are conduits through which the power and the presence of God can work, and nothing more.

There are instances when the sick individual either will not, or cannot pray for themselves for healing. There are instances when they are too far gone to communicate, and it is then that the prayer and faith of the one who is laying hands on them is essential and crucial.

Acts 14:8-10, "And in Lystra a certain man without strength in his feet was sitting, a cripple from his mother's womb, who had never walked. This man heard Paul speaking. Paul observing him intently and seeing that he had faith to be healed, said with a loud voice, 'Stand up straight on your feet!' and he leaped and walked."

The Bible does not tell us this crippled man confessed his sins, nor does it tell us he asked for prayer. All we are told is that

Paul saw he had faith to be healed. When he saw this, Paul simply commanded with a loud voice that this man stand up straight on his feet, and he did.

Whenever we lay hands, whether it is for healing, for blessing, or for power we must remember to do it in the name of Jesus, who having laid hands on many an individual never failed to see the power of God manifest through Him. We must acknowledge that absent Christ, absent the power of God in us, we are nothing but empty vessels. We wait patiently; ever at the mercy of our Master waiting for Him to fill us, for only when He fills us with His power can we in turn do great exploits in His name.

Often times we over estimate our own self-worth, refusing to acknowledge that we as individuals live, breathe and move in God and God alone. We think ourselves greater than what we truly are, and it's the one thing that gets us in trouble time and again. It is God who gives us power, it is God who gives us authority, and it is the power of God that heals, restores, blesses and baptizes with the Holy Spirit.

WE SERVE A GOD OF POWER. A GOD WHO IS OMNIPOTENT, OR ALL POWERFUL, A GOD WHO CAN BREATHE LIFE BACK INTO THE DEAD A GOD WHO CAN CREATE UNIVERSES BY SIMPLY SPEAKING THEM INTO BEING, AND THIS GREAT GOD, THIS ALL POWERFUL GOD LOVES US LOWLY, FRACTURED, IMPERFECT CREATURES SO, THAT HE SENT HIS SON TO DIE ON A CROSS SO THAT WE MIGHT HAVE LIFE.

CHAPTER SIX
THE RESURRECTION OF THE DEAD

T he resurrection of the dead is the next on the list as being among the elementary principles of Christ, though it doesn't seem all that elementary, and neither does eternal judgment, but alas, they are listed as such, and we must receive them as such. Do you sometimes get the feeling that the primary church knew a lot more than we do today? Do you sometimes feel that the primary church was closer to God, and saw more of the power of God than we do today?

This first generation of believers considered eternal judgment and the resurrection of the dead to be elementary principles of Christ. I wonder what the going on to perfection Paul spoke of really is, if these are just the foundation stones, and the elementary principles?

I want to begin this chapter with two Scripture passages that highlight the importance of the doctrine of the resurrection of the dead. Within these two passages we discover why the resurrection of the dead is a paramount and necessary teaching, and why we must fully understand and receive it as Biblical truth.

1 Corinthians 15:14, "And if Christ is not risen, then our preaching is vain and your faith is also vain."

1 Corinthians 15:18, "If in this life only we have hope in Christ, we are of all men the most pitiable."

I wanted to include both verses so we might understand a deep and fundamental truth concerning the resurrection of the dead. What Paul is attempting to convey to the church at Corinth is the paramount importance of believing in the resurrection of the dead, and of preaching a risen Christ. We do not preach a Christ who was a great teacher, an unequaled philosopher, a good person, or a prophet, but a Christ who rose from the dead. Paul realized that if Christ had not risen, then both his preaching and the faith of those he was writing to were useless, worthless, futile, and ineffective.

The reason Paul penned such strong words to the church of Corinth is because there were some among the brethren during that time who said there was no resurrection of the dead. The conclusion that Paul comes to in his letter to the church at Corinth is both piercing and of great import.

'If there is no resurrection of the dead, then Christ is not risen!'

If Christ is not risen then all is lost. If there is no resurrection of the dead, then our faith is futile, and we are of all men most pitiable. Paul was making it very clear that only by believing in the resurrection of the dead is it possible to also believe in a risen Christ.

The principle or the doctrine of the resurrection of the dead is one that is to this day hotly contested among Christian denominations, even though the Bible clearly speaks of the resurrection of the dead both in the Old and the New Testament. Paul includes it among the elementary principles of Christ because it is essential.

When we speak of the resurrection of the dead we must understand it refers to the literal resurrection of the body by God from death, and the reuniting of the body with the soul and spirit from which it was separated.

Job's simple question in Job 14:14, as to if a man dies, shall he live again? Has caused countless debates, and discussions among believers, but although Job posed this question, the Bible gives us the answer as well. The answer the Word of God gives us is undeniable, and it is within this answer that we have hope in Christ, not only in this life but the life to come.

Throughout the time of the early church, great emphasis was placed on the teaching of the resurrection of the dead, since they were certain that Christ had risen, and that they too would rise at the appointed time. It is due to the doctrine of the resurrection of the dead and the apostles' teaching it, that the first bout of persecution was ignited against the church.

What many fail to realize is that at first the church had favor with the people because they were doing good works, and many wonders and signs were done through the Apostles. It was only after Peter healed the lame man that a great persecution arose, and we find the reason for this in the Book of Acts.

Acts 4:1-3, "Now as they spoke to the people, the priests, the captains of the temple, and the Sadducees came upon them, being greatly disturbed that they taught the people and preached in Jesus the resurrection from the dead. And they laid hands on them and put them in custody until the next day, for it was already evening."

It was because 'they preached in Jesus the resurrection from the dead' that the priests and Sadducees were so disturbed. This singular topic was so controversial to the religious leaders of the time that they laid hands on the followers of Christ and put them in custody.

Why is the doctrine of the resurrection from the dead so relevant? Why is this doctrine important enough that the apostles risked being imprisoned and even killed for preaching it?

This doctrine is of paramount importance because the resurrection from the dead is the final step in the application of redemption. This resurrection will occur when the Christ returns, for it is the Christ who will resurrect from the dead the bodies of those who have departed reuniting them with their spirits. Jesus will do this, so those who believed in Him might receive glorious bodies as His now is, and go to their eternal reward.

Although this is not a study on where the soul goes when it dies, there are a few misconceptions as to where the unregenerate go to once the material is separated from the immaterial, or once the soul leaves the body and the flesh is put into the earth from which it came.

There are two prevalent theories as to what happens to man after he dies that wholly contradict the Word of God, yet are still widely circulated.

The first theory is that of universalism. In simple terms, universalism proposes that sooner or later all will be saved. During the second century it was taught that sinners would be saved after a temporary punishment by way of which they might atone for their sins, and the Universalists of today say that all men are saved, even if they don't realize it. They come to this deceptive conclusion by taking a handful of Scriptures out of context, but wholly overlook relevant passages that dispel their theory.

No, men are not saved regardless of whether or not they believed in Jesus, but only those who believes in the Son of God has everlasting life.

John 3:36, "He who believes in the Son has everlasting life; and he who does not believe the Son shall not see life, but the wrath of God abides on him."

Matthew 25:46, "And these will go away into everlasting punishment, (meaning those who did not believe in Christ), but the righteous into eternal life."

There are countless more Scriptures I can cite which dispel the notion of universal salvation, but I believe these two will suffice. The Universalists of our generation and of generations past are quick to say God is love, but they omit the fact that God is also justice, holiness, and wrath.

The second prevalent theory even in some Christian circles is that of conditionalism, or conditional immortality. What conditionalism teaches is that the soul is immortal only if it is regenerate, otherwise its final judgment will be its eternal annihilation.

The basis for conditionalism or conditional immortality is based on an artificial exegesis of two Biblical texts, one found in 2 Thessalonians 1:9, the other found in Matthew 25:41, interpreting death to mean nonlife, or annihilation at a certain point in time. There is no eschatological event in the Bible that even hints at this annihilation of souls yet men continue to teach it to this day.

Although almost all religions speak about the immortality of the soul, the Bible speaks about the reanimation and revitalization of the entire person.

Now within the Old Testament we see at least three bodily resurrections being recorded, all three found within the books of first and second kings.

The first Biblically documented resurrection of a dead person was the son of the widow woman, in first Kings 17, wherein Elijah stretched himself out on the son of the widow three times, and cried out to the Lord, praying *'O Lord my God, I pray, let this child's soul come back to him.'*

1 Kings 17:22, "Then the Lord heard the voice of Elijah; and the soul of the child came back to him, and he revived."

By way of this passage we know the sickness of the child was so severe there was no breath left in him. The child was dead, the soul had departed, yet when the man of God prayed, the Word tells us that the soul of the child came back to him.

The second Biblically documented resurrection or reanimation of a dead person was the son of the Shunammite woman who showed kindness to Elisha each time he passed through Shunem. What began as a headache eventually led to the child's death upon his mother's knees.

What I've always found interesting about this passage in 2 Kings Chapter four is that once the child was dead, the mother went up and laid him on the bed of the man of God, shut the door, and went out to find the man of God. Similar to what Elijah had done, Elisha stretched himself out on the child, and his flesh became warm.

The third Biblically documented resurrection or reanimation was that of a man whose family was burying him, and spying a band of raiders they put the man in Elisha's tomb rather than his own. When the man was let down, and touched the bones of Elisha, he revived and stood on his feet.

Although resurrection or reanimation to life was sparse throughout the Old Testament it was still documented and taught. Even with these evidences in the Old Testament, and witnessing what Jesus had done throughout His ministry there were still Sadducees who denied the existence, or possibility of resurrection. For most during the time of the Old Testament the afterlife was viewed as a mysterious thing, relegated to the mysteries which God alone understood.

As we journey to the New Testament, we see an exponential increase in both resurrections, teaching on the topic becomes more widespread through Christ's teachings, and subsequently the teachings of His disciples.

There are five distinct and individual examples of resurrection or reanimation in the New Testament, and these five do not include the resurrection of the many saints who were raised, coming out of their graves, going into the holy city and appearing to many upon Jesus' death. In case you are wondering, or you haven't happened upon this particular Scripture it can be found in Matthew chapter 27, verses 51 through 53.

Who were the five that saw death, whose souls had departed yet were resurrected and reanimated?

First on the list is the daughter of the ruler who came to Jesus, telling Him his daughter had just expired. In His passionate speech the man also said he believed if Jesus laid His hand on his daughter, she would live again. When Jesus arrived there were flute players, and a noisy crowd wailing, and after the crowd scorned Him because He had said the girl was just sleeping, He went and took her by the hand, and the girl arose.

The second person in the New Testament who was reanimated and brought back to life was the widow's son in a city called Nain. It was during what we would call the funeral procession that Jesus encountered this large crowd carrying away the dead man, and when Jesus saw this man's mother, he had compassion on her.

Jesus then came and touched the open coffin, and said, 'Young man, I say to you arise.'

Luke 7:15, "And he who was dead sat up and began to speak. And He (meaning Jesus) presented him to his mother."

Since this particular account came from the gospel according to Luke, we can rest assured Luke did his due diligence on the matter. Luke had, after all, been hired to investigate Jesus. There was enough proof, Luke perhaps even having spoken to the once dead man, that he included this account in his gospel.

Next to the resurrection of Jesus, the reanimation and resurrection of Lazarus is perhaps the best-known account the Bible offers. All have heard of Lazarus. We know he had been dead for four days when Jesus commanded the stone be taken away from the mouth of the tomb where Lazarus's body was laid to rest, and after saying a prayer, commanding Lazarus to come forth.

John 11:44, "And he who had died came out bound hand and foot with grave clothes, and his face was wrapped with a cloth. Jesus said to them, 'loose him, and let him go."

Biblically speaking, Jesus reanimated, or resurrected the recently dead, but also one such as Lazarus whose own sister Martha had said had been dead for such a long time that there must surely be a stench. The flesh had started to decompose, yet when Jesus commanded Lazarus to come forth, his soul returned to his body, and his flesh was made new.

There was also the case of Dorcas, or Tabitha, which Peter prayed over and returned to life, as well as the case of Euthycus the young man who fell from the third story, whom Paul revived after having been dead.

What is certain, is that the resurrection of the dead was not only taught by Christ, and His disciples, but was also visibly seen when God so chose to move. Neither Peter nor Paul went on from that day forward beating their chests and saying they had brought the dead to life, because they knew it was not in their own strength, it was on in their own power. It was the power of God working through them that reanimated these individuals.

We serve a God of power. A God who is omnipotent, or all powerful, a God who can breathe life back into the dead, a God who can create universes by simply speaking them into being, and this great God, this all powerful God loves us lowly, fractured, imperfect creatures so, that He sent His Son to die on a cross so we might have life.

I, for one, am in constant awe of God's love. I am in constant awe of God's mercy, and His extended grace toward mankind. How could we not desire to know more of Him? How could we not desire to know more of His power, His presence, His guidance and His will?

I would be remiss, and severely so if I did not mention the last and greatest resurrection of all, that of Christ Jesus the Son of God who rose from the dead. He is, as first Corinthians says, *'the first fruits of those who have fallen asleep, for since by man came death, by Man also came the resurrection of the dead.'*

Yes, the doctrine of resurrection is a necessary and vital one in Christianity, because as Paul so aptly put it, 'if the dead do not rise, let us eat and drink, for tomorrow we die!'

The Bible shows us in four distinct ways that the body will be resurrected.

The first of these is through Biblical affirmations of this truth, the most compelling of these being in the book of Daniel.

Daniel 12:2-3, "And many of those who sleep in the dust of the earth shall awake, some to everlasting life, some to shame and everlasting contempt. Those who are wise shall shine like the brightness of the firmament, and those who turn many to righteousness like the stars forever and ever."

The physical body is formed of flesh and blood, and is adapted for earthly survival. As such our spiritual bodies will be adapted to exist eternally with God, glorious and strong, likened unto the body of a resurrected Christ. There will be no more infirmity, there will be no more pain, there will be no more aches; we will have glorified bodies which will be in the presence of God for all time.

The second way the Bible shows us that the body will be revived or resurrected is through the declaration that our bodies are included in the act of redemption.

Romans 8:22-23, "For we know that the whole creation groans and labors with birth pangs together until now. And not only they, but we also who have the first fruits of the Spirit, even we ourselves groan within ourselves, eagerly waiting for the adoption, the redemption of our body."

The third way the Bible shows us that the body will be revived or resurrected is through the affirmation of Christ that we will have glorified bodies as His own. After Jesus rose from the dead, He did have a body, and it was made of flesh and bone.

Luke 24:39, "Behold My hands and My feet, that it is I Myself. Handle Me and see, for a spirit does not have flesh and bones as you see I have."

The fourth way the Bible shows us that the body will be revived is by the reality of Christ's return and of His judgments. When Christ returns, He will not judge the spirit, but men in their physical form.

1 Thessalonians 4:16, "For the Lord Himself will descend from heaven with a shout, with the voice of an archangel, and with the trumpet of God. And the dead in Christ will rise first."

Revelation 20:11-13, "Then I saw a great white throne and Him who sat on it, from whose face the earth and the heaven fled away. And there was found no place for them. And I saw the dead, small and great, standing before God, and books were opened. And another book was opened, which is the Book of Life. And the dead were judged according to their works, by the things which were written in the books. Then sea gave up the dead who were in it, and Death and Hades delivered up the dead who were in them. And they were judged, each one according to his works."

Although the Bible teaches the reanimation, or resurrection of the dead, Paul also tells us that once we awaken, we will have spiritual, or glorified bodies, then goes on to enumerate the stark differences between our glorified bodies, and our current physical bodies.

1 Corinthians 15:41-44, "There is one glory of the sun, another glory of the moon, and another glory of the stars; for one star differs from another star in glory. So also is the resurrection of the dead. The body is sown in corruption, it is raised in incorruption. It is sown in dishonor, it is raised in glory. It is sown in weakness, it is raised in power. It is sown a natural body, it is raised a spiritual body. There is a natural body, and there is a spiritual body."

What we know of the resurrection of the dead, as Paul continues to explain it, is that there will be a continuity of sorts, even though we will have glorified bodies. If there would be no continuity, then the resurrection would be unnecessary, and Paul alludes to this when he says 'this corruptible must put on incorruption, and this mortal must put on immortality.' – 1 Corinthians 15:53

What is the essence of this teaching on the resurrection of the dead? What is it we must understand and perceive from what the Word of God has to tell us?

First, that the resurrection of the body is a fundamental doctrine of the Bible, to the extent Paul included it within the elementary principles of Christ. When we speak of the resurrection of the dead, it refers to a literal resurrection or reanimation of the body which takes on new properties, becoming a glorified body.

The second thing we must understand is that the resurrection of our bodies is essential, because Jesus redeemed us both in body, spirit and soul.

The third thing we conclude from the Word of God is that the resurrection is possible because Jesus rose from the dead.

The fourth and last thing we must be aware of, and this truth is evident throughout Scripture is that there will be a first resurrection, of those who died in Christ upon His return, the resurrection unto everlasting life and there will be a second resurrection after the millennial reign of Christ, wherein the unbelievers, scoffers, and those who rejected Christ will be resurrected unto judgment.

1 Corinthians 15:51-52, "Behold, I tell you a mystery: we shall not all sleep, but we shall all be changed – in a moment, in the twinkling of an eye, at the last trumpet. For the trumpet will sound and the dead will be raised incorruptible, and we shall be changed."

It is the hope of His appearing, the hope of hearing that last trumpet sound, wherein the dead will be raised incorruptible and those who are still living, changed in the twinkling of an eye that makes the hardships and trials of this life seem as nothing more than a speed bump on the way to our final destination. Look for His glorious appearing dear friend, keep your eyes upon Jesus, and though trials may come, one day, and one day soon we shall be changed, in that moment, in that instant, at the last trumpet we shall all be changed, and the corruptible will put on the incorruptible, the mortal will put on immortality.

The doctrine of the resurrection as well as the Biblical evidence thereof cannot be denied. As such we must, as true followers of Christ, have the unshakable hope that one day we will rise again, to meet our Lord in the clouds. One day we will hear the shout of the Lord, with the voice of an archangel, and the trumpet of God, and in an instant stand before His glorious presence.

Our hope in Christ extends beyond this life, and it extends beyond this present earth. Our hope stretches far into eternity, because that is what our God is...eternal. In His limitless mercy He offers us a resurrection, He offers us life, He offers us eternity in His presence, and for this as well as His many graces toward us we must worship Him and thank Him in perpetuity.

GOD ALREADY HAS ALL THE FACTS. HE ALREADY KNOWS THE HEARTS AND MINDS OF MEN, AND IT WILL NOT BE SO MUCH A COURT HEARING, WHEREIN MEN PRESENT THEIR DEFENSE, BUT RATHER A READING OF A SENTENCE THAT WAS ALREADY HANDED DOWN VIA THE PRISM OF GOD'S RIGHTEOUSNESS AND JUDGMENT.

CHAPTER SEVEN
ETERNAL JUDGMENT

We've covered repentance from dead works, faith toward God, the doctrine of baptisms, the laying on of hands, and the resurrection of the dead, thus it is time to explore eternal judgment.

I realize that eternal judgment is not very popular in many of today's churches. It is given a wide berth by preachers, evangelists, and theologians alike, but it is a Biblical doctrine, one that is encapsulated within the elementary principles of Christ, and as such we must be familiar with it, and know it.

Yes, I've heard the theories just as you have. Theories that some have spawned from the depths of their bellies, of there being no eternal judgment, of there being no hell, and that all men end up in heaven eventually. Appealing as they might be, such doctrines and theories are not Biblical. They go against the fabric and the truth of the gospel, and as such they must be rejected and summarily refuted. If we hope to stand in the truth of God's Word, then we must know the truth of God's Word, and not waver from it no matter the cost.

The doctrine of eternal judgment is the last on Paul's list of the elementary principles of Christ, and I must forewarn you, this will get a little Scripture heavy. It is necessary for us to defer to the Bible, since my desire is to Biblically teach you these fundamental doctrines. It is of utmost importance that we allow the Word of God to speak to us, and not the doctrines or theories of men.

Why is the doctrine of eternal judgment important enough that it warranted being included among Paul's elementary principles of Christ, or among the foundational principles of the faith? Eternal judgment is real, it is Biblical, and it will come to pass.

By way of eternal judgment we understand God's right, through His sovereignty, to punish the disobedience of men, and rebellious angels alike. When we think of a judgment passed, a court or a tribunal, we think of it in human terms wherein men are able to plead their case, wherein they can claim their innocence, and bring proof thereof.

When it comes to God's eternal judgment, it will be more of a passing of sentence, wherein God will pronounce the final judgment, because in His omniscience all the facts are already known to Him, and there is nothing either men or angels will be able to say which will sway Him from His righteous judgments.

God already has all the facts. He already knows the hearts and minds of men, and it will not be so much a court hearing, wherein men present their defense, but rather a reading of a sentence that was already handed down via the prism of God's righteousness and judgment.

Although the doctrine of eternal judgment is highly contested in today's modern church, we see it taught and evidenced throughout the Word of God, beginning with the Old Testament, and weaving its way throughout the entirety of Scripture all the way to the last book of the Bible, the Revelation of Jesus Christ.

What we know of the final judgment is that it will take place in a future time, but in certain cases God has already made his judgment manifest on the earth. Beginning with Noah and his family being placed on the ark then destroying the earth by water, to removing Lot from Sodom then burning it with fire, to the earth opening up and swallowing Korah, To Ananias and Saphira whom God struck down in the midst of the congregation, all these were manifestations of God's judgment.

The history of the world is nothing more than the judgment of the world! Scripture shows us clearly and without a hint of doubt that after death men will be subject to judgment, because death and judgment are the two appointments none of us can miss. These two, death and judgment, are set in stone and try as men might they cannot avoid them.

From the first pages of Scripture we see the notion of judgment as a right that God reserved for Himself.

We see this truth played out within the context of the first conversation God had with His creation, telling them they could eat of every tree in the garden, but they could not eat of the tree of the knowledge of good and evil. Then God said something to both Adam and Eve, that cements the truth of God having reserved the right to judge His creation for Himself, *'For in the day that you eat of it, meaning the tree of the knowledge of good and evil, you shall surely die.'*

'If you disobey, I will judge you', God says, *'and the penalty for your disobedience is death.'*

Throughout the Bible we see God as judge of the entire earth, as well as a God of justice. The following Scriptures affirm that God is judge, and in His righteous judgment He passes sentence on the sons of disobedience.

Deuteronomy 32:4, "He is the Rock, His work is perfect; For all His ways are justice, a God of truth and without injustice; righteous and upright is He."

Psalm 9:8, "He shall judge the world in righteousness, and He shall administer judgment for the people in uprightness."

Ezekiel 7:27, "The king will mourn, the prince will be clothed with desolation, and the hands of the common people will tremble. I will do to them according to their way, and according to what they deserve I will judge them; Then they shall know that I am the Lord!"

Judgment is the action of God's mercy, and wrath in history, as well as in individual lives. God is righteous, therefore He must judge unrighteousness. God is holy and as such He judges men according to their way, and according to what they deserve. If not for the blood of Christ which cleansed us, if not for the grace of Christ which clothed us, we would be judged according to what we deserve, and like it or not, we all, to the last, deserved death. We all, to the last, deserved to be removed from before the face of God for all eternity. It is by the sacrifice of Christ, it is by the blood that was shed upon the cross at Calvary that we will not be judged together with the world.

The judgment of God can bring justice to the righteous, and simultaneously bring the deserved judgments upon the ungodly. It is the same judgment of God, having different attributes depending on whom it is focused upon.

Deuteronomy 10:17-18, "For the Lord your God is God of gods and Lord of lords, the great God, mighty and awesome who shows no partiality nor takes a bribe. He administers justice for the fatherless and the widow, and loves the stranger, giving him food and clothing."

Isaiah 4:4-5, "When the Lord has washed away the filth of the daughters of Zion, and purged the blood of Jerusalem from her midst, by the spirit of judgment and by the spirit of burning, then the Lord will create above every dwelling place of Mount Zion, and above her assemblies, a cloud and smoke by day and the shining of a flaming fire by night. For over all the glory there will be a covering."

Yes, God exerts His judgment upon the earth, and sometimes He does so through men. Throughout the Bible we see three groups of individuals through whom the judgment of God was exerted, and these three were the elders, kings, and priests.

Exodus 18:13, "And so it was, on the next day, that Moses sat to judge the people; and the people stood before Moses from morning until evening."

1 Samuel 8:19-20, "Nevertheless the people refused to obey the voice of Samuel; and they said, 'No, but we will have a king over us, that we also may be like all the nations, and that our king may judge us and go out before us and fight our battles."

Deuteronomy 18:15, "The Lord your God will raise up for you a Prophet like me from your midst, from your brethren. Him you shall hear."

Judgment, throughout history, or the judgment of God carried out against an individual or a nation, often takes on very specific forms such as war, famine, locusts, epidemics, and what we today would term natural disasters. Yes, wars are a judgment of

God, as are epidemics, as is famine and as are natural disasters. I realize we don't want to hear it, I know it's difficult to process, but these truths are evidenced throughout the Word of God. Yes, God is sovereign, and yes, God allows these things upon the earth as a form of judgment.

As we progress toward the New Testament we begin to see something new taking shape in regards to judgment. The closer we get toward the end of the Old Testament, the more the focus is shifted from God's judgment in the present, to the future judgment coinciding with the day of the Lord.

Joel 2:1, "Blow the trumpet in Zion, and sound an alarm in My holy mountain! Let all the inhabitants of the land tremble; for the day of the Lord is coming, for it is at hand."

Amos 5:18, "Woe to you who desire the day of the Lord! For what good is the day of the Lord to you? It will be darkness and not light."

Obadiah 15, "For the day of the Lord upon all the nations is near; as you have done, it shall be done to you; your reprisal shall return upon your own head."

As we can see from these passages as well as others, the closer we get toward the end of the Old Testament, the focus is placed on the day of the Lord, which is coming, a Day of Judgment and justice.

As we head into the New Testament we see the continuity of judgment, and realize not only is judgment part of God's nature, it is also one of His essential attributes.

Romans 1:18-19, "For the wrath of God is revealed from heaven against all ungodliness and unrighteousness of men, who suppress the truth in unrighteousness, because what may be known of God is manifest in them, for God has shown it to them."

1 Peter 1:17, "And if you call on the Father, who without partiality judges according to each one's work, conduct yourselves throughout the time of your sojourning here in fear;"

There is one thing I need to point out concerning the aforementioned passage in Romans, i.e. the actuality of God's judgment. The judgments of God are not limited to a future time, but rather they operate presently in the lives of men. The passage does not say, 'for the wrath of God will be revealed from heaven against all godliness', but rather, 'the wrath of God is revealed' in the now, in the present.

The notion of a future judgment is heavily accentuated in the New Testament. It is a judgment which will coincide with the return of Christ Jesus, and the Word of God proves out it is Jesus who will be that great Judge.

Acts 10:42, "And He commanded us to preach to the people, and to testify that it is He who was ordained by God to be Judge of the living and the dead."

2 Timothy 4:8, "Finally, there is laid up for me the crown of righteousness, which the Lord, the righteous Judge, will give to me on that Day, and not to me only but also to all who have loved His appearing."

Now that we've established there is a judgment, and that Christ will judge both the living and the dead on that day, the question begs to be asked, why is judgment necessary? Why is the doctrine of eternal judgment worth discussing and understanding?

There are three major reasons why judgment is necessary.

The first reason judgment is necessary is to highlight the sovereignty and glory of God through the revelation of every individual's eternal destiny. On judgment day, the principal purpose will not be the destiny of individuals, but rather the glory of God. He who sees all things, He who knows all things will execute righteous judgment.

The second reason that judgment is necessary is to reveal the measure in which every individual will receive their reward or their punishment. Once again, this is God territory, something that only God will be in charge of.

The third reason that judgment is necessary is to give God the opportunity to establish the verdict, to pass sentence, on every individual. It will be a great and terrible day, this Day of Judgment... great for those who received the Christ, who fell at the foot of the cross and repented of their sins, and terrible for those who rejected the Lamb of God, who scoffed and mocked and despised the merciful creator of all.

We must also look at the practical applications of judgment for our daily lives of faith and by doing so we will realize the doctrine of judgment satisfies the inward sentiment and feeling of a need for justice in the world. We see injustice everyday of our lives whether in greater or lesser measure, and something inside us cries out for justice each and every time. The knowledge that there will come a day when all will be revealed, when justice will be done, when the righteousness of God will pass sentence on the sin, injustice, inhumanity and depravity of this world satisfies our constant need to see justice done. We realize that God's universe is just, the Creator keeps a strict accounting of all things, and He will act accordingly. Yes, God knows all things, and on that day He will judge all things.

Looking at the doctrine of judgment from a different perspective we realize it also helps us in forgiving others because the truth that vengeance is not ours but the Lord's is cemented in our hearts.

Romans 12:19, "Beloved, do not avenge yourselves, but rather give place to wrath; for it is written, 'vengeance is Mine, I will repay,' says the Lord."

When we accept and acknowledge God as the righteous judge of all, we rest in the knowledge that He will avenge His own, He will defend His own, and He will do a far better job than we can do on our own.

This Biblical doctrine of eternal judgment also motivates us to live in righteousness, and good works that we might store up treasures in heaven, wherein neither moth nor rust can destroy them, and where thieves do not break in and steal. It is a principle encouraged by none other than Christ Jesus, and He assures us that what we have stored up in heaven is there in perpetuity. What we have stored up in heaven cannot be lost or stolen, it does not lose value, and it is not subject to inflation. It is safe and secure waiting for us to claim it.

For the unbeliever, the doctrine of eternal judgment is also a motivator to repent. It is a warning that the Bible itself declares sternly, that rather than scoff at the imminent return of Christ, and walk according to their own lusts, they ought to humble themselves and seek the forgiveness and restoration that can only come by way of Jesus.

Within the context of eternal judgment, we as children of God are also motivated to evangelize, to preach the gospel to the nations, to urge to repentance and a return to God. God's desire is that none perish, but this does not mean none will. God's pleasure is for the wicked to turn from their ways and reconcile themselves unto God so they might be spared the eternal torments of everlasting judgment.

Ezekiel 33:11, "Say to them: As I live, says the Lord God, I have no pleasure in the death of the wicked, but that the wicked turn from his way and live. Turn, turn, from your evil ways! For why should you die, O house of Israel?"

Yes, there is an eternal judgment; a day of reckoning when the living and the dead will be judged in righteousness, and in light of this truth, we must live accordingly.

I committed to writing this book because it is important for the body of Christ and for us as believers to reacquaint ourselves with the fundamentals of the gospel, and with the elementary teachings of God's Word. Only by possessing knowledge of these things will we be certain of the foundation upon which we stand, and know it is stable, secure, and above all it is in Christ.

Very soon the manmade foundations upon which many stand will be shaken to their core. They will be brought to nothing more than rubble, so only what is in Christ will remain. Only what is tethered in God's Holy Word will stand the test of the storms that will soon descend upon the world.

If any man claims to know God yet does not know His Word, that man is a liar, and He does not know the one true God. As our knowledge of God's Word increases, our knowledge of God simultaneously increases, because He reveals Himself through His Word. We cannot hope to know God without knowing His Word; we cannot hope to grow in God without growing in the knowledge of His Word. These two things are symbiotic, and the sooner we realize we need to get into the Bible, read it, absorb it, live it, and know it, the sooner we will know God more fully and completely.

The preceding might sound off topic, but it really isn't. This entire book, after all, is about knowledge of God and knowledge of His Word. The Word of God is brimming with examples of the consequence of ignorance. Due to absence of knowledge, and an absence of healthy doctrine, men even come to reject such fundamental teachings as the resurrection of the dead, and by relation the resurrection of Christ from the dead.

In his first letter to the church of Corinth, Paul spends the entire fifteenth chapter defending both the facts of Christ's resurrection as well as the importance of His resurrection. The history of the church of Corinth is well known. The people Paul was writing to had strayed from the truth and as consequence the church was heavy laden with sin. If anyone had been given the choice, there would not have been many hands raised if offered a pastoral position in Corinth.

If you've ever taken the time to diligently study both first and second Corinthians, you will have realized that the reason for all the sin, the reason the church of Corinth was so removed from the truth of Christ, is the absence of healthy doctrine. This is the selfsame reason sin is so abundant in today's modern day church. It is the selfsame reason why the church is powerless, and it is the selfsame reason the power of the Holy Spirit is not visible within the congregation of believers.

Although Paul had done his best to teach Christ, Him crucified and resurrected, others had come in after Paul's departure and began to teach aberrant doctrine among which was the denial of Christ's resurrection from the dead. Even though we have the Bible in our day, men continue to do as those of old did, bringing in destructive teachings, or as Peter calls them destructive heresies, which confuse and alienate the children of God from the fullness of Him.

In his straightforward and sincere matter Paul the Apostle of Christ, begins to dismantle every false teaching running rampant in the church of Corinth, reminding them that if we have taken His yoke, then we must walk the path He has set out for us, and not make our own path that will lead nowhere but to destruction.

It would be wise for many of today's cutting edge, modernized churches to revisit Paul's letters to the Corinthians, and see that there is but one way into the holy of holies, and the way being in the Christ, and through the Christ of the Bible. We cannot worship different Christs and hope to be welcome into the kingdom of the one true Christ. We cannot make our own path toward eternity and live with the expectation that it will lead to the same destination the narrow path of faith will. Our duty is to submit to the authority and will of God, being ever aware His Word is as a lamp unto our feet, showing us the way to a greater knowledge and greater fellowship with Him.

The reason for all this foolish doctrine we are seeing, the reason for all the deception in the church, the reason for all the sin, is our departure from the truth of God's Holy Word. We have departed from the path of righteousness, and no longer consider such things as the fundamental principles of Christ as necessary or even relevant for our day and age.

As unpopular as doctrines concerning the judgment of God might be, they are necessary for our spiritual wellbeing and growth. Though volumes could be written concerning the judgment of God, what I want to focus on are the characteristics of God's judgment, so we may discern what the judgment of God is and what the judgment of God is not.

The judgment of God will be a unique event, which will take place at a given moment pre-established by none other than God. God's judgments will be eternal and irrevocable, with no possibility of an appeal. Once God passes sentence, it is done, and the possibility of His sentence being overturned is nonexistent. Unlike human courts, wherein men get to make appeals, God's court already has all the evidence, it already knows the entire case from top to bottom, and when God passes sentence, it is always just and righteous.

God's judgment will also be an external event. God has given man the necessary time to judge his inward parts, and to judge his heart. He has given us a conscience, which acts as a warning bell whenever we stray from God's plan, and on that day He will judge mankind in righteousness.

The judgment of God will also be a visible event. Judge and accused will stand face to face, and for the unbeliever it will be for the first, and for the last time that this will occur. Yes, men will stand before God, with no possibility of hiding their hearts from Him, with no possibility of justifying their sins and refusal to repent, for God will know all, and see all.

The judgment of God will also be just and passed down on an individual basis. There is no such thing as collective salvation, and so there can be no such thing as collective judgment. Each individual will stand before God as an   individual. Each individual will be judged individually, and each one will be individually sentenced or rewarded. For the godless it will be a frightful day indeed, when they see the One they denied during their time on earth, when they will have no place to hide, no place to go, and no one to turn to for aid or comfort.

Another aspect of eternal judgment needing clarification is who exactly will be the judge? We know that the Bible tells us God is the judge of all. This is plainly laid out in the book of Hebrews.

Hebrews 12:22-24, "But you have come to Mount Zion and to the city of the living God, the heavenly Jerusalem, to an innumerable company of angels, to the general assembly and church of the firstborn who are registered in heaven, to God the Judge of all, to the spirits of just men made perfect, to Jesus the mediator of the new covenant, and to the blood of the sprinkling that speaks better things than that of Abel."

Although God is the Judge of all, He will fulfill His work through Jesus. God the Father will delegate the judgment phase to God the Son, that all should honor the Son just as they honor the Father.

John 5:22-23, "For the Father judges no one, but has committed all judgment to the Son, that all should honor the Son just as they honor the Father. He who does not honor the Son does not honor the Father who sent Him."

There are a few Bible passages that attribute the judgment to God the Father, but there are also Biblical passages that tell us the Father has committed all judgment to the Son. I want to go through a few of these passages, because we must understand Biblically the complexity of both the judgment of God, and who the judge will be.

First, we will go through a couple passages that denote the fact that the Father is judge, and then through a few more passages revealing the truth that the Father will commit all judgment to the Son.

1 Peter 1:17, "And if you call on the Father, who without partiality judges according to each one's work, conduct yourselves through the time of your sojourning here in fear."

Romans 14:10, "But why do you judge your brother? Or why do you show contempt for your brother? For we shall all stand before the judgment seat of Christ."

So by these two passages, it is clear that God judges without partiality, and He has the complete authority to judge as He sees fit. As we continue through the Word however, we see God has given the authority to the Son.

Acts 17:30-31, "Truly, these times of ignorance God overlooked, but now commands all men everywhere to repent, because He has appointed a day on which He will judge the world in righteousness by the Man whom He has ordained. He has given assurance of this to all by raising Him from the dead."

2 Timothy 4:8, "Finally, there is laid up for me the crown of righteousness, which the Lord, the righteous Judge, will give to me on that Day, and not to me only but also to all who have loved His appearing."

2 Corinthians 5:10, "For we must all appear before the judgment seat of Christ, that each one may receive the things done in the body, according to what he has done, whether good or bad."

So it is God the Father who commits all judgment to God the Son that He might judge righteously. The Scriptures also tell us of the angels and the saints who will participate in some manner or fashion in the judgment of mankind.

Matthew 13:41-42, "The Son of man will send out His angels, and they will gather out of His kingdom all things that offend, and those who practice lawlessness, and will cast them into the furnace of fire. There will be wailing and gnashing of teeth."

1 Corinthians 6:2, "Do you not know that the saints will judge the world? And if the world will be judged by you, are you unworthy to judge the smallest matters?"

As far as what the judgment itself will include, and what the principles of this judgment will be, it is once again incumbent upon us as children of God to go to His Word and discover the truth. One thing we must understand from the start is that the judgment of God will not be based on supposition, rumor, hearsay, or innuendo, but rather on truth.

Romans 2:2, "But we know that the judgment of God is according to truth against those who practice such things."

Nothing is hidden from God's eye! There is nothing men can do to shroud the reality of who they really are before an omniscient God. All His judgments will be based on truth, and for some the truth will be a rude awakening indeed.

The judgment of God will encompass what we did in this life here on earth. It will also encompass the words we spoke, the thoughts we thought, and all things will be brought into the light, all things will be made known before His holy face.

Revelation 20:12, "And I saw the dead, small and great, standing before God, and books were opened. And another book was opened, which is the Book of Life. And the dead were judged according to their works, by the things which were written in the books."

Matthew 12:36, "But I say to you that for every idle word men may speak, they will give account of it in the Day of Judgment."

1 Corinthians 4:5, "Therefore judge nothing before the time, until the Lord comes, who will both bring to light the hidden things of darkness and reveal the counsels of the hearts; and then each one's praise will come from God."

God's judgment will also be impartial, and it is one of the principles of judgment to which He will adhere.

Romans 2:11, "For there is no partiality with God."

If we believe our lineage, our service, our charity or our giving will somehow sway God into overlooking sin not repented of, if we think just because we were related to a famous preacher, or an evangelist then God will give us a pass, we must revisit this verse in Romans, meditate upon it, and see the truth which lies therein. There is no partiality with God dear friend, 'for as many as have sinned without law will also perish without law, and as many as have sinned in the law, will be judged by the law.'

The last principle of God's judgment I want to cover and this may be controversial to some – but it is nevertheless Biblical – is that the judgments of God are in accordance with the measure of light we possessed. 'To whom much is given, much is required,' and this principle carries on into eternity.

Matthew 12:22-24, "But I say to you, it will be more tolerable for Tyre and Sidon in the day of judgment than for you. And you, Capernaum, who are exalted to heaven, will be brought down to Hades; for if the mighty works which were done in you had been done in Sodom, it would have remained until this day. But I say to you that it shall be more tolerable for the land of Sodom in the day of judgment than for you."

In His rebuke of Capernaum, Jesus says something we must not dismiss or ignore. He says if Sodom had seen all the miracles and all the mighty works Capernaum had seen it would still be around; it would have repented and therefore not have been judged of God. As such, because those of Capernaum had seen the power of God and did not repent, because they had seen the mighty works and it did not compel them to seek a closer walk with God, it will be more tolerable for the land of Sodom in the Day of Judgment than it will be for them. Because they were shown much, because much had been revealed to them, God will require more of Capernaum, and judge it more harshly than He will Sodom.

There is one overriding truth we must take into account whenever speaking of the judgment of God, and that is if we judge ourselves now, if we look into our hearts, if we look at our lives subjectively, if we repent of those things we know we ought to repent of, and weed out those things we know are harmful to our spiritual growth, then we will not be judged of God.

Rebellion is always at the heart of our unwillingness to repent, to bow our heads and bend our knees and humbly ask the eternal God of all for forgiveness and restoration. The Word tells us rebellion is as the sin of witchcraft, something God abhors and detests, and if our rebellion keeps us from judging ourselves, if our pride keeps us from seeing ourselves in the light of God's Word and acknowledging our need for forgiveness that can only come by way of the blood of Christ washing us clean, then yes, we will be judged together with the world on that great and terrible day of the Lord.

We are, all of us, given ample time to repent. We are, all of us given ample time to receive and accept the grace of Christ freely given to those who open their hearts and see themselves as God would see them. If we choose the way of disobedience, if we choose the way of rebellion, then we will most assuredly be judged, because our God is a holy God, our God is a just God, our God is a righteous God, and He judges without partiality.

The world seems to be falling apart around us. Those who are to be representatives of Christ in this present world seem to have been caught up in the things of the world, the love of many is growing cold, and the truth of God's Word is being dismissed en masse. We are witnessing unprecedented times. Times of upheaval, and heartache, times of trials and persecutions, but it is in these times the power of God must be all the more evident in the lives of His children. It is in these times that the power of God must be all the more evident in the lives of those who claim Christ as Lord and King. It is also in these times of uncertainty and chaos that we must know our foundation is sure, and we are standing on the rock of Christ. We must realize that we know we have received all there is to receive from His hand, that we are equipped for every good work, and the spirit of God dwells in us. Only then will we be able to walk in the victory He has promised us.

The fundamental doctrines in this book are a good and solid foundation to build upon, but from here, we must go on to perfection.

Yes, we can walk in the holiness of God, yes we can walk in perfection as Paul calls it, because if it were not so, then God would not have demanded it of His children.

'Be holy, for I am holy' said God; 'be holy in all your doings.'

If He demanded it of us, then holiness is attainable, if He demanded it of us then holiness is achievable. It is only when we consider ourselves wiser than God, dismiss His Word, and discount what He has commanded that we see the yoke of Christ as heavy, and not light, and the narrow path of faith as difficult rather than easy.

It is not burdensome serving God. So serve Him with gladness of heart.

ABOUT MICHAEL BOLDEA

Mike Boldea was born in a small northern Romanian Village. At the age of nine, his entire family was deported from Romania for smuggling Bibles. His grandfather, Dumitru Duduman started an outreach ministry called "Hand of Help" of which Mike is now Chairman.

Mike has traveled internationally with Dumitru for over 11 years acting as Dumitru's translator. They shared their testimonies, as well as an important message God gave Dumitru for the United States.

Recently Mike has translated the book entitled "Life In Christ" which Dumitru had penned prior to his death. The testimonies of those that were persecuted for their faith must live on to build up the body of Christ. Mike continues to operate in his gift as an Evangelist to exhort the body of Christ to present itself with a garment clean before our Lord.

Michael has a strong Christian heritage coming from a line of four generations of Christians. In the village of Hinceste Romania his great grandfather was one of the first Christians converted there and his grandfather was a pastor and his father pastors the "Messiah" church in Botosani Romania with over 800 members. Their family worked with Richard Wurmbrandt, Harlan Popoff, and brother Andrew taking bibles to the underground Church.

Michael has seen the presence of God in accomplishing the work that his family was called to. In the face of great persecution and opposition thousands of bibles were given to the Christians of Romania even though it was punishable by imprisonment if caught. His grandfather, Dumitru Duduman did suffer greatly being imprisoned for his faith. Under extreme torture he never recanted his faith and stands as a witness of faithfulness to this day in Romania.

ABOUT HAND OF HELP MINISTRIES

The Hand of Help Ministry was founded by Dumitru Duduman in 1986 in a small apartment in Fullerton California. Brother Duduman was a Romanian pastor who worked many years with Brother Andrew's ministry smuggling bibles into Romania and Russia before being exiled to America. Brother Duduman and his family, out of obedience to the Lord, eventually returned to their homeland and with the help of American supporters have raised up an effective ministry which continues the work to care for God's people in Romania. Here are some of the outreach programs sponsored by Hand of Help Ministry:

The Hand of Help Orphanage is located in the Romanian town of Botosani. The town has 90% unemployment which has caused great hardships. Many children come to the orphanage because their families can no longer take care of them. The orphanage currently cares for ninety orphans. The Hand of Help ministry is able to clothe, feed and offer a helping hand to the children because of the gifts that support this ministry. As you browse through the Hand of Help web site you will see the smiling faces of children who now have hope. They are loved and taught the Word of God. Please consider helping or sponsoring one of these precious children. If you want to learn more about sponsorship please e-mail us at handofhelpoffice@aol.com.

Over the years the Hand of Help Ministry has offered an out-stretched hand to the community. Families have been sponsored to come to America to re-build their lives. Other families in the area have been helped by receiving food, clothing, medicine and much needed financial gifts. Each year containers of goods are sent to the Hand of Help orphanage to distribute to children and families. You can be assured that your gifts are greatly appreciated by these humble people. The government is not able to provide the necessary funds to care for those in need. They must have our help. The Hand of Help Ministry has programs which specifically support the community. For more information you can call Hand Of Help Ministries at 1-866-371-7636 toll free.

More than fifty churches have been built and funded all across Romania by the Hand of Help Ministry.

Made in the USA
Lexington, KY
03 January 2014